Best & Sandra:

Thank you for

Shards

the support

of

vie Patreon

My Soul

and for

(The Fountains of Fortitude)
(The Third Three Fountains)

helping

with the books.

I hope you both

Robert J. Koyich

get to

spend more time off

and with eachother.

Love, light, & luck!

Peace, Robert.

DEDICATION

To my soulmates, it's explicitly true I can never be you.
Yet in some ways, you know how to be me.
May we always know how to have and share PLU8R as a key?

CONTENTS

Sand to Silt: The 9th Fountain

THE THIRD ROUND

I don't think people yet understand the puzzle I've found myself within. There are very different and divergent layers of disparity in my awareness. Some have a home, a job, and in some cases a car or truck, and in other cases, even more of an abundance of income. It contrasts those with near nothing.

Regarding income, I know that I have less than most people who have a full-time job. I also understand I'm blessed and have access to more than some people. Some cannot receive PWD (disability) as I do, or even welfare and also need support. There also are people that work *and* receive governmental benefits.

The people that have jobs and an income of $24,000 a year are earning more than I had in 2016 and 2017. For those that made more, I wish you can create and acquire even more ethically and allow some for those that want improved lives and situations. When we have money, we can make a more significant impact depending on how we use it.

I haven't always worked a regular hourly paid job. I do, though, put in a fair deal of effort and work. Some would laugh at the idea that writing can be a viable career or profession, or that it's work, yet much is required to bring books into the world. Many levels of skill, commitment, and devotion are needed to form a book, and I *have* chosen to work on a creative pathway.

As of May 2019, I'd not yet earned much money from writing. I deem the role and function of authorship potentially quite valuable, even beyond earnings as there are intrinsic gains of self-awareness and learning. It may be great for others to write their books too, and for those that do, I hope you find the benefits and increases in your results also.

Some may wonder why I don't have to work a full-time job

like they have to. I agree that PWD is for people that can't function well at work, and I am a person in that situation. Some people on PWD contribute in different ways, though, and even when unable to work full-time, we can bring value and connection and be positive influences.

I know from past jobs and experiences that I'm not capable of working forty hours a week at a job. My near-violent reactions by being held or trapped in work positions are not a benefit for anyone, and I'd lost my sanity and composure previously when working. As a dishwasher, I freaked out, and I went nuts working at Wendy's too. I also couldn't tolerate some behaviours and spiritual energies when I worked graveyards at a gas station.

I've sometimes found myself barely able to cope with being alive. It's tricky to be responsible and be employed when mental health issues hound. When I wrote *Fields of Formation,* the 5 Fountain, I was pushed far to the edges of safety and sanity. I'm incredibly thankful and fortunate to be alive, and though it may not seem it, my life has been difficult at times.

I have what I have, yet some aggravation from others may exist because I have the grace and blessings that they don't. Or, it could be because I don't work a job I hate as some do. My thankfulness may not be entirely understood or appreciated, and though I may not have things like a car, I'm grateful for what I have.

I've often had concerns about what others think, and with the disparity between myself having a home, food, and water compared to those that don't, it makes me want to help form a balance. I choose to provide, though my work hadn't yet earned myself a primary living income for myself, let alone providing for people in our community.

I've attempted a creative salary through authorship and music, and by using the sales of books and music as a pathway to earnings, my efforts and merits shall hopefully result in a win/win. If I can share my work and earn money by selling books and albums, I commit to sharing some of those earnings.

Shifting to personal relations and people we know, many like to be our friends and not just contacts or customers. Of Gary Vaynerchuk's statement, "marketers ruin everything," I'd still like to find a balance of engagement and genuine care coupled with the ability to earn prosperity. By now, the people that love me as a person, and don't want to read what I've formed, may be put off by me marketing to earn sales.

If I establish a livable income from my creative endeavours, it's a fact I've not marketed well up to this point. I've spammed some people with my ideas and the concept of Providing Point (my charitable work and cause), and I don't want to work full-time as a fundraiser.

The big hairy audacious goal of Providing Point is to provide food, shelter, and water for *all* people. I've started with gathering for and from the people in the town I live in, though it seems like a completely irrational goal. I understand the models and theories for future growth, yet with results up to May 2019, we hadn't grown significantly.

It's a humanitarian viewpoint to believe that people should all have their basic needs met, and perchance our prosperity does manifest. I've denied my guilty conscience from loving my life, sometimes, and I wish others could adore theirs too. It sometimes seems, though, that something isn't right.

An additional difficulty I find myself in is that it doesn't matter what I want, it's what others want. If others want to be negatively irenic and aim at me for being too ambitious, or oppositely lax, then why is it okay for others to have materialistic or other grand wants or do nothing themselves?

If I desire basic human decency, safety, and a solution for all, how could I achieve that on my own? I'm not definite that I can. I've vented and expressed negative emotions and have had angst because it seems I'm going nowhere, yet what I want to do is encourage others to delve into theories and ideas for a more cohesive unity.

If I can propose a solution and articulate it for others to hear or read, though, what would it matter if no one else understands, listens to, or supports it? I see the distribution of my books as seeds that can be shared and planted in other people's gardens, and it does start at home. I need to sort out my attitudes and behaviours and let the books provide awareness and new thought. I know I can't force people to read or care; it has to be an open invitation.

If my ideas and recommendations encourage others to share and foster positive reciprocation, then isn't that an additional layer of good? Dare we find this work as a conduit for the benefit of many? If I set myself aside and work for others again, shall we find ways to advance our understanding and process?

The seeds sown germinate to sprout and grow in the gardens and fields. If I revert the ideas upon themselves, it's then my responsibility to plant, develop, and tend the soil. If these ideas and creations are the seeds I believe them to be, then I must trust in others and share them.

Some seeds or plants may never fully flourish, yet I think it's worth planting. We may grow some fantastic things, and though it may be presumptuous to think of harvest too soon, perchance it is a law of numbers thing again; plant more seeds, and more shall grow.

As part of this, I fear a penance and retaliation for not pushing for pledges or sales. If the objective is to provide for people, then why have I not marketed more vigorously for patrons or sales? If I develop ethical marketing skills and don't abuse awareness, can we achieve some radically good results?

The intent, purpose, and function of the books have shifted a lot since the first book, *Finding Natalie*. The obsessive path of sharing my cliché wishes and whims also shows my ideas strafe me away from conflict. I also sometimes dislike hearing myself speak, and even if not to the same people, I repeat myself a lot.

When I write, I can form elaborate ideas and thoughts, and it's a lot easier to read and write without interruption. Instead of hearing me chatter obsessively, people can process if they want to, or not. A book is also more permanent than a conversation. Another massive bonus to writing a book is how the mind and thoughts go on cycling, tripping up, and dissecting time. It's a fantastic learning process.

We can share one coherent linear view and sequence, and welded insecurities can guide us to prune and edit the dominos before toppling the series of text you read. You give me a chance to carry on and forward with the process without having to always connect to telepathic assailants.

The delicate dance of boundaries and ethics challenge me to participate, and when some people are crucially inceptive, there can be a dance instead of a fight. The footsteps of the dance are tracked on the screen when I write this as some may be invasive or offensive without even knowing it.

If we are put into an uncomfortable or defensive position, and not by a physical threat, it may be a reactive nature that instinctively lashes out or scrabbles for self-preservation. I have my shortcomings and faults, and I know when someone pressures or attempts to coerce me into things, I have become reactive or reluctant.

We may shift attitudes and actions with autonomy. Space to make our own choices and decisions often finds the correct results naturally follow; especially as we develop ethical knowledge and principles. I don't always know what is right and accurate, though, and when I find errors in my thoughts, actions, or words, I must become aware of them and adjust.

As I acknowledge my mistakes, even when some think it foolish to do so, I must accept my transgressions. Secular repentance holds a dangerous edge, though I hope writing and processing my faults is helpful and not my folly. Admitting mistakes is a stepping-stone to atoning and adjusting behaviours.

I also need to speak up more often. When there are transgressions about others, we can feel how we shift paths. It's tricky, though we can guide others to make good choices. If I'm wrong and repent, I can change my actions and pathways to develop forgiveness.

What do I hope for you? First, I should know who 'you' are. As these books have formed, I've sometimes written to specific individuals, yet the pronoun 'you' can be used as a general outwards inclusive word. It's also true that when we capitalize the Y as You, that a religious context can bring God into the meld.

I value inclusion and note it's a unity word. For those who've not encountered my writing, I should mention some of the base bridging principles and ideas I use. PLUR is a primary one from raver culture that signifies peace, love, unity, and respect. I use an '8' in my version (PLU8R) to include many other R's; the first three are responsibility, representation, and reciprocation.

We can't yet know what happens with the books, and I can't always tell you when they'll be complete. I can, though, work towards completing this book and others. Building towards the future, we learn bit by bit and grain by grain. We gather, hone, and meld the shards, and even when done this book, there is a lot more to write. It's an involuted process that takes decades to cultivate.

WITH THANKSGIVING

I think my life is like a soap opera sometimes. I'd prefer that far more than it being an action or horror film. I've had a concern about organized crime and plots and plans aimed at me, yet there's also a lot of care and love for and from some characters in the drama.

Cued from the keyword 'drama' I also hope and wish that my life not be a tragedy; I'm not a tragic hero. I learned what the word hubris meant in class the previous semester; it's excessive pride or self-confidence. I've had a concern that having arrogance could be a fatal flaw, yet cleaning some of my innards and bringing faults to light sheds away some from my being. My books are part of my journey and process to clean up some behaviours and thoughts.

It was Friday of the 2017 Thanksgiving weekend when I first started writing this chapter. I was inclined to write a chapter about what I'm grateful for and a Lewis Howes webinar that week reminded me to live in gratitude.

I'm so exceptionally thankful that I'm alive. I also carry ideas and a foolish faith and belief that some good will come to Earth through me writing and recording. I'm dearly glad that *The Sands of Yesterday* formed and that the primary commitments for giving rose in that book.

I shouldn't build a house on sand, though I remind us that sedimentary stone is a thing that also may become metamorphic; I'd like to use the book to show the transformation.

The saying of 'water under the bridge' means that the debris from above is carried down the river to return to the ocean. I practice carrying gladness and thankfulness with me and open up parts of myself that I may not like, yet also parts that I need to understand. I use my writing as self-help and healing as, up

7

to now, I think I do need an actual therapist; I have traumas to process and accept too.

When I formed this, I was without a direct mentor, though some online mentors and their lessons guide me. Their experience and advice share much as they teach valuable skills and ideas. People like me who haven't had money for their products and services must remind them their work is appreciated. I thank them each for their generosity of love, knowledge, blessings, and wisdom.

Gabby Bernstein and her book *The Universe Has Your Back*, is a recommended link to those that are searching for clarity and spiritual understanding. I first suggested *The Universe Has Your Back* to a friend nicknamed Emerald Sprite; a dear, kind, bright, and bubbly friend. I wanted her to find the lessons Gabby shares to bolster her faith.

Gabby's sign is an owl, so I bought a stuffy owl to relay to Emerald. She passed on it, so instead, I gave the owl to Opal Sprite, a different rad and super-kind friend. Some of the lovestones (gals that are loved) have been so incredibly kind and welcoming to me, and they're dearly appreciated. I value their humane treatment of myself and wish them amazing lives too.

I'm also thankful for the Magic shops in town. Two of the shops have let me sort cards for credit and are places where some pretty rad people meet and gather. I have a boundary of not spending money on a Magic collection again. I ran myself into bankruptcy in 2015 by spending extravagantly on investment cards and irresponsible spending. I sold all of my cards, though I miss the friendships and contacts made at the shops.

I've not acknowledged my parents and family here yet. Adjectives would cheapen how appreciative I am for my parents, yet I'm also happy that one of my cousins backed away and gave me the space to live my life. I appreciate family and know I've not reached out to some of them so much. They may or may not feel the neglect.

I've sometimes felt sad and remorseful about forgetting or

neglecting people. If I spin that to a positive, though. If I feel bad that I've overlooked or ignored some, it reminds me that those people matter to me, and I care about them. Sometimes it may be best to let others live their lives without jumping into their worlds though.

I feel relieved my evolving awareness shifts to stay on positive notes, waves, and energy more recently. When I become conscious of adverse or invasive tendencies, when something or someone is terrible for me, shifting to authentic goodness can be a positive habit. It's pretty cool to be able to acknowledge bad things and source positive behaviours from them.

In *From the Valley to the Fountain*, the third Fountain, I talked about smoking and how I benefit from tobacco. I learn vital truths and gain pleasure from cigarettes, though I note they're not something I would ever recommend. I'd like to know how to quit, though as I formed this, I still was a smoker.

Truth is a thing too, though reality's not always bright sunshine. Differently, Emerald Sprite commented about how she thinks people are becoming more accepting of each other. It's rad when people don't try to control other's, though exhibit self-control. I think I need more self-control and that I need to give more grace and forgiveness.

If I can evolve to be less judgmental and more supportive, I also must remember not to condone some things. Acceptance and forgiveness of others and ourselves is a fantastic idea that can lead to grace, yet when things are not okay, we must do something. If we can accept life and learn to appreciate and acknowledge our actual merits, we can both prune our faults and bolster our positive qualities.

I like and love that I've seen the value of people working and holding jobs. Some have earned trips and vacations, and some have been able to buy things they want. Some too have had luxuries to enjoy, such as meals at restaurants and vehicles. People have earned these things; I haven't yet.

When I talk about charitable ideas, some say they like the concept, though few have signed up with a pledge to Providing

Point. The few that have pledged are helping support others with grocery cards, and I'm appreciative of their generosity. I also see kindness with books when some have paid for books even when they know I would have shared a copy for free. I like it when people want to give and not take as much as they can for free.

Many people that I've offered books have said 'no' too. I'm entirely okay with a 'no' when I present a book to someone. If they don't want to read it, they don't like me, or they honestly have any other reason not to read a book, I accept that. As some mentors tell us that asking people is okay, the ability to be okay with a 'no' is also a precious ability.

I'm thankful I have my basic needs met, I'm glad I have a home, food, and water, and I'm fortunate to have a computer. I'm pleased to have a bus pass, I can go to school and Toastmasters, and I'm grateful I even have books to read and share. I see many ideas for a combined Freedom Solution, and I'm thankful my attitudes have shifted a lot in the past couple of years. I work for a unified, shared, and positive understanding.

I am, though, baffled as to why I'm allowed to live in a first world country. Although some people complain about the government, I'm a person that values the systems and services that the Canadian and provincial governments have in place; they allow me to live the life I live. I may not be above the poverty line according to national or provincial standards, though my life is so incredibly abundant in many different ways.

I'm also very fortunate to have learned some ethics vital to my wellbeing. If I can assist others with their lives and not have to push so actively, it's brilliant. I'm thankful to have what I have, yet it can't all be only for my benefit. Some online mentors tell us that if we earn more, then we can share more; I like and value that idea.

As my earnings increase, I can do far more for others, my family, my friends, and myself. There is a wealth of time that I'm also thankful to have, and as I'm learning how to manage my reality, I work to assist and keep open to accepting a strengthening of gratitude. It's pretty rad!

Appreciating something and acknowledging the same thing are keys to gratitude. Something can be recognized, though gratefulness includes the appreciation of it. It results in a feeling, a positive attitude, and twists in an equation idea.

Awareness + Appreciation = Gratitude.

I have materialistic wants too, though I see how we can use things and money as a channel to provide for more than ourselves. Two examples? If I have a car, I can drive people to places and connect friends to future locations. Two, since 51% of the earnings from my three-part book sales go charity, selling more books means more money for me too.

It's clear if you've bought this book that you've given monetary value, though the additional benefit you provide is to allow us to become who we are. As I have the chance and opportunity to experience all sorts of life, I put a few lessons and ideas into the text with this work. My books allow us to gather seeds formed throughout the preparation of each Fountain and other publications.

If I get money aware again, I think of how so many other people work so hard to provide so much for the people that cannot. Some people believe in welfare, PWD, and a basic living income, and the people who pay taxes or have bought these books have helped with providing for those in need too. Thank you! Not all are thankful to do so.

When this book first started, I was at a point of frustration. I was ticked off and agitated by the fact that other people are angry that I'm happy and thankful. I'm aware some people are mad at me, and it seems few want to help us. Our Freedom Solution is when we *all* can find financial, emotional, mental, spiritual, social, and physical freedom. It's not a rational ideal, yet a worthy goal.

Socially, we need to be in contact with people, yet solitude can hone the mind and find other benefits. The kindness of a shared visit holds the value of inclusion both in the past, the present, and also the future. When we gather with people to interact, work, or play, we can enjoy them and be appreciative of their company.

A friend named Stella was part of a painting group. Stella formed a painting with vibrant colour and was part of an experience with people in an engaging activity. Gathering in shared groups can enhance our lives, though it extends in Stella's case by sharing her painting with friends via Facebook.

Stella received many loves and likes on the posts showing her pictures, and I hope the comments added to her experience and brought her happiness. When we share our passions, love, and likes and mean them, it's a way to contribute to others. Positive comments can lift a heart, and add to the remarkable fact people care and like what we make. The twenty people at Stella's event held a shared experience of painting, though the beauty expanded.

Magic: The Gathering is another part of my life and communal activity. A Magic friend named Ryan visited my home and showed me how to create printed proxies of the cards. Ryan gave me the benefit of learning how to create proxies so that other players can play Magic with cards they don't yet own or can't afford. The Magic communities I know are pretty rad people, and Magic players know that people matter.

I want to make sure we can add and not detract from other's wellbeing. The accumulation of time, knowledge, and experience are part of how we evolve, yet some things are like an instant. They change the entire game and sequence of events and can cause immediate ripples outwards. Some other stuff, though, can be like a glacial structure built and developed through gradual acquisition and take years.

As we learn to encapsulate our fragmented moments of gladness as a memory, we also may think of the future technology that transfers our consciousness. Imagine experiencing the entire perceptions of another being from their point of view; appreciations, awareness, and thoughts planted directly into our mind.

If we can give a hug, a kind and genuine compliment or gift, we can share generously with spirit at almost any moment. We can behave with kindness, goodness, and truth and infuse beautiful things, attitudes, and energy into life. Some notions can solidify fantastic parameters, and preparation for future events and people we've not yet met are ideas to consider.

As with our appreciations for others, if we adjust our actions, attitudes and intents, we can slowly or quickly gather some perfect moments. We also can secretly plan to surprise people with seals of love and security, and in one moment can choose to be for all and not just ourselves.

How will you act and behave to work for the betterment of life? For what are you glad that you have that you want to share with others? What experiences or wisdom have you gleaned that you can recall and recount to another? Would you like to demonstrate appreciation to those that you admire or love? How?

I hope you are glad and thankful for your life too. If you're reading this book, you have the luxuries of time, the ability to read (which includes sight, access to books, and a mind to process), and also the ability to appreciate another person's awareness. Good things can cause happiness and peace, and we can do some pretty rad things that we may have believed we couldn't.

Even if I've not yet met my gal, I don't have a car, and I have so much time without communication, I also know I'm building a future. Even if I haven't yet sold many books up to this point, or can't even imagine providing for myself let alone a thousand people, I'm thankful to be alive. I'm fortunate to dream and be grateful that we're here on Earth.

Please remember that for which *you* are grateful. Please learn to be thankful and gracious for anything or nothing. If you can learn to approach situations to be okay and grateful for any outcome, better results may occur and be much more appreciated. Miracles can happen far more frequently, and a consecrated effort can help improve results.

Remember those who help us and those that need our help. If we have compassion and a willingness to provide, we can improve lives and many outlooks like ripples. Saying 'thank you' is a key phrase to remember to keep on the tip of our minds and our tongues.

With that in mind, thank you. Thank you for allowing us to be, even if we cannot yet see. Thank you for reminding me to be like a drop of water in the sea. Thank you for allowing us to free the devotions held within the glee, and thank you for reminding me the world of Earth includes seven billion other humans, including the allusions to Bri.

HOLD THE BOND

If I'm to stay true to this chapter's title, then I should clarify which bond I mean. Some connections are lingering covalently, yet electrons haven't exchanged. There are people that I like and love, though I'm not so keen on being locked into full contact with some of them. If I'm not even clear if I could stay stable with another in a living confine, have I been like a hydrogen atom who lost its two neutron pets?

When we spin different substances into water and create a solution, we may find ionization. I've treated myself very much like a free agent or single nodal point, yet I also wish not to be so noble. I want to be allowed to interact and also not be dangerously reactive.

We can consider ourselves out there in the ocean of life, yet be right and sure there is some salt in the expansive network of being out there. There is much beneath the surface, and no matter how calm the water looks, experience, resources, and activity are abundant.

On a molecular scale, the base protons and neutrons bind in the nucleus of an atom. I like the idea that there are a bunch of positive particles held together in the nucleus, yet recall they're often with the neutral neutrons with electrons blitzing around the core. According to physics and chemistry, there is no room for a negative particle in the heart of an atom's nucleus.

Maybe we should heed the laws of nature in the metaphors of our lives and not annihilate. It may be some view me as a negative electron that's not allowed into the core units of other's atoms. I could be part of that negative cloud orbiting them, though I also think of planets and their orbits around their stars. The moons and debris around a world can blend in a multitude of distant suns, and how we spin around the central node of time is like the centre of a galaxy.

There's an introduction to *The Simpsons* on episode 14 in season 15. The opening holds an animated sequence that spans outwards from within the inside of the family's home to a view from the outer atmosphere of Earth from space. The animation's perspective extends extended outwards beyond Earth, past the solar system, and then, far outwards of the Milky Way. As the view scans further out, the many galaxies became the particles of atoms, following into compounding as the building blocks of DNA. From the focus on a strand of DNA, the animation expands outwards to show a body's cells, and then the camera comes out from Homer Simpson's head. The picture on the screen then displays the family sitting on their couch, precisely from where the camera's perspective had started.

Relationships of family, a link of communication, and our consciousness hold perceptual knowledge bases. We, as individuals, know other people, animals, plants, or things can change us and that if we become aware of anything, those objects can change our thoughts purely by being part of our consciousness. If we are in another's awareness, we have affected the context of their mind.

I hope you see how you react when another tries to bond with you. Others affect us; especially when we like them or want them to love us. These desires can cause complicating things to happen, though. If we draw in and attract those that dislike or feel cynical about us, we shall need to choose how to respond. If we can't stop adverse reactions, though, how can we assure we're not harmful if we're negatively affected?

Time can dissipate hate and also be a buffer to minimize the result. If we know we are going to explode when put with another, we can be responsible and keep away from connecting with them.

There are people and things we like and prefer, though. When we bond with them, some bonds will only hold briefly, and other relationships may solidify forever. How can we secure a positive outcome with those we like or enjoy? A few may not be suitable or proper for us, yet what happens when we become magnets for the fantastic things we want and enjoy? What happens when we attract miracles after adjusting our polarity?

We test and learn to know how we'll feel, think, and respond. We can experiment by being with someone over a more extended period and assess the experience. Think of someone that you've liked on first meeting, and then later found yourself wanting to repel them and the very thought of their existence. What of those you've held dislike, and then later wish they never leave you and your life? It's a very particular concept and a genuine thing.

If we are drawn in and attracted to another person and they don't want to bond with us, there are times where we may have forced the connection. I'm sure you've understood this; when we've liked a person a lot or felt drawn to them, some of them have then later been 'meh' or even cynical about ourselves. Not all people want to connect. There are others too who have desired to bond and connect, yet we didn't want them to.

My mind goes to the intuition of fission and fusion and how they're also metaphors. Fission (splitting) makes me think of how an unstable nuclear compound separates the atom and makes two entirely different substances. Fission reactions also produce a lot of heat and radiation that can be unhealthy for life. This type of nuclear reaction can be like a nasty divorce; it's mighty, affects many things, changes fundamental properties, and also may have started with an unstable material.

What I'd like to find is the *fusion* relationship. When two lighter atomic nuclei form a solidified meld, and a new compound arises. Fusion may cause the creation of intense and powerful energy, and I'd like to shape a full synthesis of the idea in a different book. If I form my lifelong mate through fusion, though, with who shall it be?

For those that know part of my story, we know I'd gotten very focused and transfixed upon a famous singer who is almost entirely unknown to me. Natalie Imbruglia was my obsession and focus for many years and very clearly the central fantasy I held for a significant portion of my early adult life.

The first Fountain book, *Finding Natalie*, was initially intended to be shared with the world and lure Natalie to come and meet me. I had soul stalked her, though, and still, it shows that decades after my first awareness of her, I forced a bond with a person who didn't want me. I put a lot of attention upon her and was trying to push the process to meet her. I don't even know if she knows who I am, yet I've had ideas she does. That's where my written journey started.

Today, I'm aware I have been inappropriate with my words, text, attitudes, and behaviours towards many and not only Natalie. From the start of this chapter, I also know I cannot claim, wish, or intend to choose the one to bond with forever. I don't want to put a scoundrel like myself towards one that holds my heart down and up from the vaults of my life. Natalie best not be sought out and used as a goal no matter what my truths are.

So if not to pick her, I also must remind myself of the reciprocate; what will happen if another chooses me, and I don't want to bond with them? How will I react to another person has thought such outrageous thoughts as I had for Natalie? Is that type of person on Earth wishing and yearning to meet me?

From the side of famous people, I wonder how they cope with so much attention and focus on them. It's especially tricky when they're honestly only known through media. Within a Petri dish idea, on a level of biology and not chemistry or physics, what is happening when a bunch thoughts, nature, and exposure starts to seep outwards? It develops a culture and maybe how we're forming mould and not a seed.

Twisting in further with the word 'culture,' I think about music and how Rap and Hip-Hop is a precise, pervasive, and robust culture. What if such a dominant culture view me as an enemy and wish to withhold or condemn my expansion? If I got ejected from working as an emcee, perchance that's why I got moved to the authorship dish.

What happens with my strains of thought that are alive? What of that brought into the awareness of those who wished me removed? What about those who work to develop their practitionership and thrive within the game, and my thoughts are fuel? Am I seed, a mould, or a weed? I find myself at a crux where I feel concern about how juxtaposed some time and ideas mix.

Back to chemistry, if people interact like different chemical compounds and contact with elements create new things, sodium in water is an example of how some combinations can be dangerous. Differently, some connect and gel strongly and positively with others, and in full and constant contact can assure a stable and unbreakable bond.

For myself, I have spoken of wanting a girlfriend, yet the past fourteen years has had me living without a roommate or girlfriend. Other than when I had two cats, the two neutrons I referred to earlier, there's a metaphor for how I'm a proton in my nuclear family. I may be Hydrogen.

I joke about religion now in that I could say that God is the Oxygen atom that splits itself, yet add the premise of Ozone as the Trinity. Trusting in God and Jesus as the living water in combination with us as individuals should not forget the Spirit. It's how the three of them together prevent those on Earth from being torched by UV rays.

Oxygen fused with two Hydrogen atoms forms water, yet, according to the Chemistry theory, the two Hydrogen atoms are bonded to and separated by the Oxygen atom. Rewinding to the fission idea, I think I've been attempting to fuse to establish Helium. Maybe water is a better objective? I honestly don't know.

Electrolysis is the process where electricity separates the chemical bonds of H_2O into Oxygen and Hydrogen gas. If we separate water back into Oxygen and Hydrogen, pairs of atoms return to their connective parts; O_2 and H_2. I wonder if we find that elusive fission to make a nuclear family, or am I destined to fuse with others in a pair as water, ice, or steam.

What shall the Fountains do, though? They are links to

water, yet if their molecules separate with electricity, shall the particles connect people like I suppose they may? With one friend's feedback on *Seeds of Tomorrow*, she found the book optimistic, honest, and empowering. Forget how I want to bond; what about others and how they want to bond? Remember too, in this analogy, there are many elements in the full spectrum of life. There are one hundred and eighteen elements in the periodic table.

With couples, I'd like to find ways of strengthening some of their connections. I never want to be the reason that a couple separates, and with some relationships, there have been points I'm concerned commitments could erode. How do I help them hold the bond?

My parents each went through two divorces. It was their second marriage that resulted in me, and even though they both fundamentally changed their lives through their divorce, I feel like a released particle after their split. As I'm an only child, I think of how I could have been an Oxygen, and they were my parental hydrogens as the first waters of my life. It happened that I stayed with my Mom, and my Dad connected with another.

Seriously, though, what if I am like Oxygen. Two bytes (16-bits) of information held within one shell of a body. I can interact with many different materials, though lots of people don't like rust or things exploding or being put on fire.

As things affect my consciousness, maybe I should ship off from the chemistry and work on psychology. If we remember salt also helps convey the messages through the neurons, I think we could send a different synaptic result. I don't want to bleach things, though I like to keep things clean.

I don't know what solid ideas bond in your mind. Perchance that's why I write; to cause new connections with the linear directions of text. I want to connect with the future, and if I was to be with one specific lovestone, it could have been Uranium split, and the three neutrons scattered from the reaction could've been our kids. The separation would produce a lot of energy and radiation, and we'd be changed.

I've fantasized that if Natalie and I married, she'd eventually want a divorce anyway. Our three kids would be scattered with their energy causing other separations, and I don't want to split up like that. Is it best, perchance, that I stay as a single proton in my nucleus if I wish to have a core family with unity.

I'm still unhealthily over-obsessed and self-focused, though I'm also thankful I hone in on and dissect the shards. I may have some of the worlds against me, yet as I make secular repentance, I reveal and discover what my faults and follies are. I must become aware of my mistakes before I can comprehend, accept, and process them.

I hope others find their books too. The incredible insights and attunement from the ability to write are so vital for those who want to know what life is all about. Through forming these books, I've tossed ideas and thoughts off and onto the Internet, and I've dug into feelings that have shredded my heart while compounding my soul.

We may show positive consequences, though, because, at this point, I remind us there are forces of above, below, and all around us. There are parts of realms I've never experienced, though they tell me that many people, compounds, and experiences have already bonded.

Some bonds endure an last, though, and for some who have passed away, they'll always be attached to the psyche of another. Ghost particles are also legitimate and part of a spiritual realm not covered in this section.

Regarding becoming aware of things, it's often easier to do so when we are isolated. If we can separate ourselves from the others who are either forcing or attempting to bond with us, we can become clear about who and what we are. I know I'm not an inert gas; there are substances, people, and materials to connect with. Perhaps it's a conscious element to pervade.

CHART A COURSE

Friends are valued and beneficial for our hearts, so I learn to remember that more often. Two friends had just dropped me off at home before I started writing this section; one is a male friend codenamed Jund, and the other is his girlfriend. I don't know her exceptionally well, though I know they both are amazing and rad people.

The change from faith to fortitude cues us forward to build a solid base. The title *Etched in Stone* shows the shift in my inclinations from my past two or so years. I had not achieved very much success with the bookwork or sales up to 2018, though knowing that also sets my intent and actions forward. I regather my life and work and have faith in the higher powers of Earth and the cosmos.

My book *The Sands of Yesterday* leads to remind I need a firm foundation like bedrock to build upon, not wishes, whims, and fancy. If I am to create foundational work, then I must secure it upon a rock-solid faith and system of universal life that is not just what I want.

My rested faith in our future must be explicit before it ensues. There's power in making claims, commitments, and proclamations, though they must be backed up with action; one cannot claim to do things and then not act. Almost always, nothing will magically happen without effort.

The ideas of putting in the reps or honing one's craft are vital, though we also must couple those activities with other endeavours. While strengthening value, I've planned a lot and put out points of purpose and relationship, yet have lacked some of the first crucial steps.

Regarding my books, I have written a bunch, though haven't formed pitches to sell them. I may have made some progress through the maze as the first few dots connected.

Often mazes have an explicit entrance and exit, and if the metaphor holds, the entry could be the fixation I carried about my dream girl. My wish is the end of the maze is past the year 2053, and I'm in the room where I need to discover the secret places and pathways to navigate the middle of my labyrinth.

The vision of my home, the Glass House, is one of the focused points of my future life, though I need to pass a great many aspects in time and multiple corridors to reach there. If I get to build the Glass House, then I must get my books to market and sell them.

I hadn't yet known what value or purpose the content of my Fountains books have for readers. Selling books must be a multi-win, and I've yet to understand why people want to support those wins. Although I'm not clear of the wisdom of the idea, the question is: "What would happen if I made myself famous for generating sales?"

I'd achieved notoriety in Vancouver when I was trying to be a rapper/MC, and that path almost led to my death. I know some of the reasons for that plot and plan linked to my drug use and how I showed an obvious lack of morals. I was projecting myself as being far more significant than I was, and I also was deplorably out of bounds with my thoughts, actions, and attitudes. I admit I breached and abused many boundaries.

Some people understand my lack of control and mental issues and that I also have authentic merits. There's a reminder a few people do love and honour me, and I know this because I'm still alive. I have, though, polarized communities in the past because of involvement with different cultures.

With my current bookwork, I have an idea that my books hold value for others if people read them. How do I get people to understand that and process them? At this point, I've found that a very few have read the books and that those that have are people that like, care, or want to support me.

If there is value for others in the books, I don't know yet how to articulate that to another. With the fame idea, I incept the concept because I know some of the value in the books is because people know or have an interest in who I am.

Is this a double-sided piece of the puzzle? That if people read the books because they know me, they will understand more, and that people who want to know who I am will learn? I paralleled this with movies in a conversation.

Some people will watch anything and everything from a director because of who the director is. Some other people will watch a film because of what the movie is regardless of who the director is because it's a good movie. My idea is to create books people will want to read because they are both exciting books and also because people want to see what I've written.

I don't so much want fame, yet instead, I am plotting and planning what we can do if attaining popularity would facilitate the channel of book sales. If I can continue to create and live, maintain my principles and commitments, and grant grace and prosperity, then how I can convey these ideas to others as something people want to support?

It's almost like I *have* to push for being very well known to allow the Seed Fund, the Glass House, and my self-sustained income to be things that manifest. My awareness narrows my view down to how can I achieve those goals.

The answer is to form a plan and start taking the steps. This chapter is processing that and where I stemmed the title *Chart a Course*. My first instinct is to describe what the books are, though they're all about my thoughts and me. Who's interested in that!? I seem to believe that it's not so many people.

Do my books land in the self-help section? No. Do they tell people how to run a productive business? No. They indeed don't demonstrate how to improve one's health, how to fix issues in a romantic relationship, or even how to invest one's money. The Fountains books don't even explicitly teach others a valuable skill such as how to write, how to market services, ideas, or products, or even clearly show people how they can find success or their dreams. I haven't relayed explicitly valuable skills or formulas for others to follow or use.

What my books do convey, though, is a series of thoughts that insight one to think deeper about some social issues and other concepts. My books hopefully shall instill a bit of compassion and kindness, and by discussing some of the frustrations and fears I have, a few delicately placed ideas and points of knowledge can incite people's understanding and hope.

I glean much by forming these books, though how can I encourage or invite people to see what they hold? I'd become so well known in the past through the channel of music and got ejected from the rap game that I think I may be tainted goods. My reputation from the past still holds fragments and shards seemingly aimed at my heart and mind.

I know I didn't succeed in the Rap game and that I'm not suited to live in that ecosystem. I'm not an extraordinary socialite with levels of confidence and skill required for surviving there. The hate and animosity aimed at me caused some of my fear and insecurities, and I don't often feel so brave or bold.

If I hold away from the world because of my cowardice, though, how will I comply with the will of God and stand up for many more than myself? I'm inclined to think I'll stand up for some, yet how does sharing books with people support that belief? Books are a more suitable channel for conveying my thoughts compared to music, though how are my thoughts valuable?

The path of authorship is far different than the music game and suits my more introverted personality. I set my wants aside sometimes, and twist and turn guidance into the fuel for our future. My fear of condemnation has had me wishing to break free of almost everything, isolate crucial points of fact, and find a positive way of empowering much more than myself; doing so in a peaceful and prosperous way.

I hold value in fairness and have a belief if I'm to gain readership, I need to risk becoming very well-known again. How will I learn, act, and behave as we move forward to generate Full Seed? What I write may be openly scrutinized as I come from a past where written words hold far more permanence. I've grown much since living in Vancouver, and even if I've carried corrupted thoughts, my ethics secure.

There's a line in a recording made by friends in Vancouver that said: *"Make it through to the knowledge side… Natalie, kids, and a dope-ass ride."* I know that music is prophetic, yet did that 2001 reference mean that I'd shift from making music to what I'm doing now? The line secretly calls my delusions back with a blend to remind us I still don't know.

What if *The Sands of Yesterday* is put into the crucible and melted into a new form? Would it be glass, or can we dare return the sediment into stone again? What if we allow all the *Fragments of Intent* to cement the heart back into where it formed? It's not the same piece of work, yet what of Kintsukoroi? Can we fabricate something even more beautiful from the fractured remains?

How can something be etched in stone if there is no rock upon which to carve the words? Is text the time muddled in a metamorphic heart? Are these shorelines of writing a process of something which to weave, deceive, cleave, or leave? If we are brought forth as being eternal, who else shall ever believe?

Is it true that it's a stone upon which my thoughts etch instead of rock? Why is God the rock? I should build on a reliable foundation, yet I'm still not clear if my fountains have eroded parts of the truth away.

I've bathed my being in the waters of life while neglecting to remind myself my work is like a glacier. Mountains *are* rock and stone, though dare it be I'm skiing on a glacier separated from the foundation? Has my job kept me away from knowing God even though it's stability for which I yearn? Maybe I should stop skiing and dig deep into Earth.

If Earth is where God's humans are, is that where we're helping The Universe with our past, present, and future? What if God doesn't want me on this planet? Christians would say that 'let God's will be done' and that we should accept that. How can one condone another for wishing life to be entirely removed? If God created us, then why would he design us to insight so much hate, contempt, and distrust? Have I been set up for defeat, or is there a secret plan?

If we are to chart a course, then we must know where we

want to go. That's where my future wishes and wants are my guideposts. I hope to find kind people that can welcome my ideas, and my challenge is to know where to be, and then question how to get there.

Who *are* the ones that will help us sort out a collective Freedom Solution? Initially, I wanted to use the Seed Fund as a promotional idea to generate sales as a win/win idea. It held that people would be more likely to buy my books if they knew it funded a charitable cause. If people want to help, though, they can give directly with more efficiency.

The manipulation tactic of having people buy my books to have the Seed Fund thrive was partially self-interested. Andrew was right; it seems pretty scummy. If I shift my reason for pushing sales to be for personal gain, is that a more socially acceptable strategy?

In chapter eight of *A Distant Glimmer*, I made an income declaration. I made a hedge because if I committed 100% to Providing Point of *all* my book earnings, I would be working for 0% personal gain. The final choice was heeding Gary Vaynerchuk's advice and putting just over half of the profits to the cause; 51%. If to sell something, though, the product or service needs to be valued and valuable.

How can I tell people that the books are valuable beyond what they generate financially? That's where I wish not to be deceptive. The ability to sell is vital, though according to my ethical wants, I'm intending on earning my audience through trusted recommendation. I prefer that we generate interest and acceptance in my work and let it speak for itself.

It's a glacially slow process, though as my books are so much about my ideas, and not marketable knowledge or advice, the results up to now have been awful. My foolishly optimistic self still grasps at hope and fate that the books hold purpose, though if my compass guides correctly, and we draw the map correctly, why would anyone go searching for treasure if there is none?

The focus should be on giving, not trying to sell the map to people or trading for the compass. These books are a map of

SHARDS OF MY SOUL

my life, and your responses and guidance are the compasses. I should make sure to plan for the compasses to help guide us towards a treasure as we traverse the map.

SIAMO INTERNAZIONALE

I love Earth, I appreciate other cultures, and I love languages. Life carries our truths forward, and as I write, I find that there is strength in shared beliefs. My values of inclusion and multiculturalism infuse different languages, though I've sometimes used them to obfuscate.

From a deeper understanding and appreciation of my core self, I may sound vain or obscene. I like the people at Snowpeaks, the Thursday night Toastmasters group, for how they remind me how Earth holds many different people from so many different countries. We can learn about how to speak and interact, though I need to learn other things too.

My work includes many more than a few, and though I'm the one who presses the keys of these books, each edit layers. I use Introversial as the banner for my work, while the Fountains books have been the primary projects. At this point, I'm the only person working as an Introversial artist, yet the Fountains are public.

With awareness and connotation held, some may admire a fountain; there can be statues to adorn them, yet not all should drink the water. On travel, I've seen fountains in public squares in Italy that benefit the towns, yet in 2017 and early 2018, Snowpeaks was a square that brought me an essential and keen public place. I prepared a speech there titled *The Seed*.

When I was a member of Snowpeaks, Japanese, German, French, Portuguese, Spanish and Dutch were represented with three Spanish speakers from three different countries too. It reminds me how language crosses borders. The Thursday night group members all interact and speak in English, yet I was the only one of two whose first language is English.

Language and culture is one way to remind us that we're not alone or the same with our comprehensions. Think of locational differences between people, like how we can start at home locally or provincially, expanding nationally, and then even globally. As the human population was in 2018, we're bound to Earth, yet that might not always be the case.

My Dad and step-mum live in Australia, and when I was in grades five through seven, my Mom, Dad, and I lived in Hong Kong. I don't know Cantonese beyond an exceptionally few simple words, though I loved living in Hong Kong and it was a radically good experience. I want to visit there again, though I also lived in Australia, and that links to how I'm thankful to be allowed to be there too.

Even though I'm a person who's appreciative of different cultures, drugs corrupted me. My thoughts and insecurities put barriers between others, and myself, and I'm still learning to cleanse my mind. Revealing parts of my psyche that mayhap should be hidden, I've had a scary issue with racism.

I don't like racism, especially the slurs, the hate, and the violence stemmed from it. I've been aware of and exposed to some racial issues, and those experiences had tainted my thoughts. My theories about telepathy include premises that not all of the ideas in my mind are my own, though some of the worlds would contest that. I also don't want to blame my mental corruption on drugs, though I know that they have played a substantial role.

The doubters and believers mingle in the Contialis. If I'm to argue with the doubters and spin in my self-analysis and self-awareness, my thoughts twist back to how love is the solution. I believe that by learning more of my absolute truths and, as I recommend to you, writing them down, might help clear up some confusion.

I wrote in the book *Built from Within* the night before. It was a stressful evening, and what I wrote sourced from my insecure and doubtful side. I mentioned how we can control our language in different ways, and how it's easier to write our intended meaning than it is to speak sometimes. It's also easier to manage our spoken words than our thoughts, yet our truths may spill out through Freudian slips. The subvert twist, though, is that it's our thoughts that can have the most potent effect on our lives even if we don't speak them.

We live with our thoughts every day, and if I hold my written work as a way to share myself, my written words are more secretive than my thoughts ironically. Few know my written truths, yet many have assumed things about me from what they've heard. With my firm belief in telepathy, I wonder how much of Ashley's opinion is right.

Ashley believes that our body language carries a stronger weight than what we say. She also thinks that no one else can hear anyone else's thoughts. I've differently thought myself to be a psychic beacon and additionally believe that thoughts and feelings are manipulated easily with sensitive thinkers. There are knee-jerk reactions we may feel about things and physical, emotional, and mental reflexes are a particular thing. Maybe it's what people see of us when they are approaching and not our thoughts?

As I live on my own in my apartment writing these books, I'm often alone. When living in the thought realm and having no one to talk to, it's difficult to escape from some thoughts when I get diverted onto a negative thought train. I have no ground wire to dissipate the negative static electricity of my mind sometimes, and the friction of life can cause a buildup of energy. The impulsive releases of energy are sparks that can shock a mind.

We must be aware that Earth needs to be a well-oiled machine and that communication and positive reciprocation lubricate our beings. I believe that things can change our attitudes, and though it's electrical, the idea of magnetism holds a different polarity. It's best to recall that gravity and nuclear bonds exist too.

All these electrons are coursing through the water of life, and if electricity, a flow of negatively charged energy, can separate water into the separate Oxygen and Hydrogen gasses, we must be careful. We could cause an explosion by igniting the Hydrogen when it's in its gaseous state while the oxygen could aid combustion.

Gravity holds liquids in their containers, yet the seriousness of the issue is that I think I often miss my cue. We are digging deeper into the layers of our life by allowing me to nudge the cursor right along the page continually. Are the Fountains shifting and changing directions of the loom that she weaves; asking Jordan too if the Red Sea finds the freshly fallen leaves?

Water is life; that's a universal Earth thing. We don't know if other planets need water to live, yet it's an assumption. This planet holds water as one of the most vital components of life as we know it, yet that's where I shift back to humans and the structures we've made. We've built a world where ideas and information have accumulated.

Some ideas recycle, and some are stored away in our histories unknown. Some other parts of life are held within the realms of vague ideas and awareness and have zero mass. The notions of time and space carry the purpose of the spirits and souls that have died also and hold substantial importance. Theoretically, they too hold no physical mass. An idea or thought with no physical form either shows we know these things can change matter.

Systems of culture and religion are omnipresent, science is ingrained in many culture's reality and belief, and the concept of business is also inherently linked to human dynamics and interaction. In a cognitive monetary system, humans are the dominant species regarding technology and stored or recorded information. We also know some ideas of life don't track money, science, or belief. Living in the animal kingdom is instinct, intuition, and action and is still eternally linked.

I'm pretty daft actually. Because I'm a human and have a computer to type on, I have been abusing the ability to infuse my ideas and theories into the minds of another. If our thoughts build from instinct, our words and language layer upon our beliefs, and our desires guide how we attempt to manipulate life, then I remind myself to trust myself and use my words for good. The idea to work for good is a biased idea too, though. Where does the source of life come from that assures that people are aware of what I think, say, do, or write?

The astronomers say there are millions of galaxies and billions of years beyond and before us. Others have said there are infinite Universes that exist outside of our mixed reality, and if you perceive this in any way, even if not yet in a printed form, you are alive. That also could be a lie. Perchance you haven't been born, or you are a spirit of one long dead that attunes to the magic.

Where my language blends in is partly sourced from an international game, Magic: The Gathering. Shoulspeak also is an Earth idea, though not known by many people. The codes I use include colour referencing and a compelling notion of perception, yet Math is also a prevalent idea. Earth combines geometry and hopes into principles that understand other worlds; even if consciously in the non-living spirit world. Shoulspeak is a combination of some of those ideas.

The downside about language is that only those who understand or know the words they read, hear, feel, or speak will comprehend them accurately. It may be my responsibility to learn, yet I also intuit, even to my chagrin, that it is also my responsibility to teach.

Our ethics may change, and the changes in our values shall also affect how we communicate. Sometimes I may be alone, though I put my trust in a faith that we shall evolve. We are responsible for our own choices, numerous influences direct our decisions, and it's a choice I make to elaborate on our lives. That's partly what my books do.

By setting objectives, I may not achieve them all, yet I make the goals anyhow. They give me a point to direct towards, and I accept some ways of life may never be known. There also is the truth I won't do some things and that once something has happened, it's happened.

Do we get to choose what we do, or are we each following our own predetermined linear responses of time? Reacting to our perceptions, our views sequentially guide us towards some explicitly non-avoidable points. Or, do some entirely unchangeable things allow us to hone our pre-conceived ideas into ever present moments holding awareness of the climb?

Have we already passed the moment that just happened and are never allowed to experience it again? We at the very end of time moving into the next moment, which is gone forever, into a new present that is now the past. What happened when time travel took us back to before now to live the moment again? Déjà vu?

Or, are we floating along in our shells of bodily awareness, gradually understanding that they set ideas from the galaxy in a teardrop? Is emotion only an animal thing? Do non-living things not hold psychic energy by being aware of other living creatures? Do we as humans function only to unearth the truth?

Am I able to start this sentence with any other word as the second word in English and still have it be grammatically correct? Do you dare them to be eternal? Who can assure it to be true? Certainly not myself. I am a human who is often baffled by the idea that I am.

It's an intentional lure to make us think; I don't often try to invoke thought. I know, though, that I do. Who is the first name that you remember? Who is the most recent person that you thought of afterwards? Is it the same person? *"We can't talk about that"*-Cam, of Division G.

What of the Round Table? Is the Arthurian legend known across cultures? If we only understand or comprehend English, how shall we communicate with those that don't? There are some words in English that everyone knows that I never want to hear or think. Some words are spoken too often that no one has ever imagined, yet some people have never felt anything other than that. "I love you."

What if we live as if our entire being is already known? What if what we don't know about ourselves is right and we never come to understand; until we meet another who reveals every one of our truths. What if what we think is untrue is fortified fact? That's where our communications can baffle and befuddle.

I recall my auntie Bonnie saying: "What if we all think you're an ass, Rob?" I know I've indeed been treated like one. What if you are pure, amazing, awesome, and real, and no one will believe you? What happens if the involution of all things of an unknown being is brought into our awareness? What can I tell you? What truths can I convey? What if you don't know I exist?

I still don't know.

Shape our world. Hold your love. Share. Create! Learn? Yes. We must. Know too that we may never know, yet that you know, and also that you may always remember.

"Of all that I have remembered, I haven't forgotten a thing."
--Cliff Roulston

It's straightforward to focus in and be aware of nothing but oneself and one's own thoughts. We're not solo, though; we are each a central node of a conscious being that is part of multiple cosmic realms. Though this chapter's title says 'we are international' we are not just that. We each are part of everything; all things, thoughts, entities, matter, and time are part of a whole. It is wise for us to remember others and the fact that we're all integrated.

We share a universe. It is diverse, often definite, and divine, *and* it's not just for us alone to know. Get out there into the world of Earth and sip in some of the fresh waters. There may be some things yet for us to learn and share, however too, there is an exciting twist of our planet; perchance some other species would like to visit here and have, yet are not from Earth.

I'M IMPATIENT

From a review of *Finding Natalie*, there was advice to form the books as I had started them; as a journal. In line with that guidance, it was December 10th, 2017. I am eager, yet there's a layer of repentance also; I've not done enough.

My actions have pushed some away, and I've used some people. I've been impatient with the results of my work and have an edgy feeling of not knowing where to put the plow. I can write, though that might not be enough. There needs to be a definite purpose and intent to result in Full Seed; providing food, shelter and water to *all* people.

I don't think my heart is deep enough in collaboration with many to achieve complete coverage, and there is a time-sensitivity too. Each day I'm not providing additional resources for others in need is another day that someone is going without. Even though Introversial's Patreon earnings go to others, if we didn't have contributors, then what may we give?

I'm so impatient with my school, work, and process! I had an exam the next day and was on the computer because I was too agitated about my situation not to form this. I want to market, earn, share, and seed future yields, yet I've not gleaned many sales or pledges.

As the Fountains are partly my processing journals, I've written some of the plots and plans in them. The advice is to share the schemes, ideas, wishes, and dreams with others and write this here. School is beneficial, though finding out how we can achieve Full Seed has a time pressure and stronger importance than overpreparing for an exam.

The situation compels me.

The books must have value for readers beyond just the function of what their earnings do. What lessons or ideas can we share that will improve many lives and not just our own? The premise to give is vital, and it's an ethic that holds. What my need is is to provide value and earn the right to be read. My work must have value beyond a functional purpose to supply people with resources.

Some people don't want to force others to learn what to do while people thirst for knowledge or ideas they've never heard of or read before. Still, some others may yearn for a story to read and escape from their lives. What my wants and wishes are isn't enough to be used as a channel to persuade people to help a cause; as far as I think.

The desire to give others ethical principles may amplify compassion and kindness, yet that requires kinship with those ideas and prerogatives. Knowledge is a seed of its own, and as much as I can't just wish for others to align, I can nudge some others onto pathways for positive forward motion.

The invitation to read a book is another challenge. With books, it's not just a monetary investment or a give; the time to process them is another thing. It must be a win/win. If you've given me your time to read what I've formed, there best be a gain for yourself too. If the books are so much about me, then how or why will that have value for another? Who cares and has an interest in this work and process?

My attempts at being poetic or insightful are not a strong lure either. The actual derived value may even be not what I write, yet instead who I am and what I can do for the world regardless of my books. A desire to earn a productive life is overtly money-focused, and my passion for works and words have an impact that seems like a fruitless effort.

An objective to share is to find our Freedom Solution. Our Freedom Solution of doing what we want to do with full financial support veritably has been the impulse of these books. Even if my promises are for others, the primal urges and sources of these books is impatience and dissatisfaction with how life is.

Finding Natalie was my dissatisfaction with decades of unresolved feelings, *Searching for Tomorrow* was from malaise with not knowing my path of life, and *From the Valley to the Fountain* was from my impatience with reaching the goals of the first two books. I fueled *Seeds of Tomorrow* with the displeasure of disparity and wishing for results, *Fields of Formation* stemmed from being unhappy with how life was mid-2017, and *A Distant Glimmer* was me pissed off that I've not done more. Now, in *Etched in Stone*, I've been frustrated I've not accomplished more results from the creation of the books.

Remember this, though, we find ourselves in the present and can be grateful to remember we can make a new start. Many ways of forgotten days pass into now. I know some people still need a home, and if we can't use my books to find homes for some of those people, then why do I do this?

My personal needs are few, and *I* don't need to worry about what I want. I have my coffee, my ciggies, my home and I have my friends, my family, my work. What I do need, though, is to remember is that I can help our communities in ways other than shelter, resources, and books. If I can share some good ideas and conversations about how to build, help create, and develop understanding and compassion, then those may be values worthy of conveying.

Ask yourself some of these questions please? How do you like helping people? Do you prefer to help people with their social or emotional needs, or with resources? Do you want to support one or a few people, or help many? What do you have an abundance of that you'd like or love to share? What can you give today, or in the future? Would you prefer to give your time, your knowledge, your attention or your direct personal support?

Do you want to be recognized for your contributions, or are there ways you can secretly help? Are there other people who need or want your help? Though some may not like it, I do add; in what way, if any, would you like to be compensated for your help?

Do *you* need help? With what do you need help? Have you asked for help? These are three different questions that don't always come from the opposite side of the fence. Some people may seem not to need help from anyone, though genuinely require it. I also remind myself, some people may look like they need help and not want any from anyone. I mustn't assume another would wish to accept support if offered.

The question of "Do you need help?" can open pathways and doors for guidance to arrive. I think we may need to ask ourselves those three questions again. Do we need help? With what do we need help? Have we asked for help?

What if someone does need help and has explicitly asked? Both sides can view this question; the one who needs support, and the one who has asked for assistance. Sometimes people ask us for our help, though how do we respond? Do we look for excuses, or are we thankful to have the ability to help?

What of those times when we don't ask, and someone tries to help us? It's not always appreciated. I mustn't be so arrogant or assumptive that another needs my support or advice, and I also mustn't be a fool to think that I can't do more to give to other people.

My impatience lies in that muddle. I'm not clear on how I can help those in need if I don't put in a substantial effort. I put my work out into the world to allow others what they need, though, for some friends, a conversation is what they need. For some other friends, maybe the way I can help them is to give them some space and leave them alone.

If we can't or don't want to help with resources, we can find other ways to support. We can engage with others and help them with their dreams, and we can use our care and knowledge to encourage them with their work and projects.

We *can* bring ideas and connections together to network for a combined future. We also can bridge the space of time between our checkpoints and lives by sharing our hearts. Even though I'm isolated and separate from so many things and people, I refuse to give up. My bullish and persistent mind and soul refuses to stop and not forge new pathways and points of thought.

My written work hasn't yet gained a vast readership, though I intuit I must surrender to the process while still planting future yields. Though I can feel sad that I've not earned so much for others, I continue to progress and persevere. Honestly, I wonder how much of this passion, obsession, or obligation is purely neurotic and should be written off.

What are your creative endeavours? Do you write or record things? Do you draw, sing, or play an instrument? Are you a person who deems themselves non-creative? Do you cook meals or organize events? Are you a public speaker or coach? I'd be quite surprised if you're a business person reading this, as you'd probably focus on your business and not my books!

For an inverted part, are you a person who thinks collectively and are hearing the channels of thought from the person who is reading this book? My bizarre notion even knows that some of you are not yet a person who is again on the same plane of existence. There are other forces at work on Earth that are not from our galaxy.

Am I too allusive to the realms of thought not yet formed? You may not have read this whole book yet, yet know parts of it as it developed. I also want to assure what you've learned from it didn't even exist in the printed form until months after its inception.

Maybe you've read the entire saga up to and past the next book *Open to Fate*? That may not have been able to be true yet, though we also don't know what the future holds. I hope you have some wishes that have yet to unfold in 2019 and beyond as well.

I'm impatient, yet optimistically persistent. I know I can't forecast what happens with these books, though I keep them evolving and refine them. I revised *The Sands of Yesterday* again in 2018, and at that point, *Fragments of Intent* needed to go through a rewrite too. In July 2018, I was okay.

Others may not understand I know this process is going so slowly. We've yet to earn money for others, and the Purpose of Providing Point still is to provide. It calls my heart again to the fact I've not yet housed others.

What would happen if I gave up entirely on working on these books? What would happen if I relied solely on the

Universe to do that that it will? What if I yield entirely to doing what I intuitively deem best for only myself? I don't want to take that path. I need to keep making forward motion for life.

The Universe and world of Earth make good use of my creative instinct and hone the right connections. I think that fate and destiny link much of this. What if I only typed what my soul yearns for until the point of 2025 when we reach the inner walls? What if the devotions I've made are actually in the suit of heart and not the spades as believed to be?

What of the crows who assure peace holds? What of the dove that seemed to neglect my forgotten love? With a full breath, I hold the gull to pull the Kookaburra Max into the flax and keep the tracks in the racks of the packs. I'm impatient about much as I haven't flown far away from that moment of above.

There can be Heaven on Earth, yet I heard that angels are not divine, that they are merely God's servants. I thank God for allowing me to know there is a subtle union that chains me to tomorrow, yet the rhymes would say the three feathers may not be from the same species. I give them to her anyway.

How can I claim these Fountains to be of Fortitude? They still seem like Fantasy. Should it be Yesterday, then Faith, then Fortitude, and then Fantasy? I need to be secure to reach my fantasies as a real thing and apply the yesterdays that build faith and form endurance. The Fountains help move us forward and into our future.

We allow now to be then again when the signs of life seem to guide us into what I should say. I can't assure I meet my wife; no matter who she is. The pull between creative integrity and artistic freedom find the waters reveal some concealed snow and ice. It may cause some people to slip and slide, yet I also best not perform doughnuts in the parking lot.

Of the planets, Venus is said to be the bringer of Peace while Mercury is the messenger who's closest to the sun. I was to call her Aeris as my Mother would be Earth, and the Father is sometimes called Mars. It's a twist with my family that my mother is an Aries; I noticed Aeris is an anagram of that.

I doubt my future and wonder if I'm just an extra. When we see movies, countless people don't have a speaking role, yet the movie crossover also reminds you I don't necessarily want to be a star. I don't want to have to act, yet if I do compete for 39 days, I'll need to develop my ability to see through the lies. That may still be a cube of ice to chew.

Of the most primary people in my life? What does it matter to you? You maybe don't even know I exist. You may be one who's believed in me before I believed in myself. Primary people for me include my step-parents, yet I don't like playing favourites. My cousins are cool links, yet I'm distant, and uncles and aunts hold a part in my heart too.

It seems I put my friends after my family. It's weird that most of the people I can meet up with and interact aren't family; I have no family in town. I'd like to include some that I've not met in real life too who have influenced me with their music, books, online work, or guidance. I've known *of* so many, yet *known* by so few.

Many I've not yet met that hold amazing and monumental influence on Earth, yet I best not compare. Though, I've thought to have the audacity to write what I have, how could I believe that I'd ever meet a famous star and provide for thousands other than myself? I've not even been able to yet provide for myself!

Another miracle, though; I've already written what I have and have been alive long enough to record 250+ tracks and put books online. I've been able to live long enough to be here to type this. If I'm afraid that God wanted me dead, I would have died a long time ago.

What if they erased everything I've formed? What if we achieve my bold claims and audacious proclamations? What if my fears, insecurities, and paranoia are needed to plant the fields in the Universe? How do we allow my plow to be pulled ahead by myself living thirty or forty years further from now?

The consect still holds a grasp on myself and what I do. I cannot express this enough to you. It's not funny what some tell me, though it moulds me well outside the tides of thought.

Some others allow us the fact that both Heaven and Hell vie for the pacts we use to counter the spell. How shall we dredge up the secrets that you need to know without tipping the balance? It's a well-woven sequence of life, yet perhaps I need to be more patient.

IN FAITH OF OUR TRUTH

1:21 AM on December 21st, 2017. It had been a super-trippy night. I was working on putting *Fragments of Intent* online, and a message from a contact that I don't quite know sent me a note that deeply concerned me. Their message inclined the belief that the world was going to go to chaos, and they thought we should prepare for a full disconnection from 'the grid.'

I was frightened, and it carried me through some other parts of my cowardice. I know I pray to God, and I also am terrified not only of what happens on a global scale, though even on a cosmological level. I work for the Kingdom of God, though I cannot claim that I want to fight.

As I was in-depth editing *The Sands of Yesterday* I glimpsed some awareness of the Creator. I work in different ways than most, and I also understand I'm explicitly a vassal and not one in control. That causes me to fear too. I know that I'm not one who has power over God or others, and I have concerns about some of the forces on Earth.

If I were asked to be a primary leader for a great many people, I don't think I would want such a responsibility. I serve people, I don't rule, though I do write and record. I work for many more than a few, and I also know I'd prefer to provide for many than be part of a battle.

Though my lack of knowledge is extreme, I put my faith and wishes to the higher powers of the Universe. I have an intense fear that my loyalty to God, His Son, and the Spirit might not convey or align with how I also have a desire to honour other forces of life, including differing religions. That is where I see my weakness. I deem that my faith might upset some who don't believe in God by a different name, and I fear condemnation for my belief system.

I wish to learn more about other religions as they are all part of Earth. Earth is where we are, and though we need all people, a difference of religious beliefs is part of the conflict I'm concerned about on this planet. Forces such as famine and wars over resources and power are issues I can't resolve from my single point of a wish; peace in every nation, love for every race, unity of every creed, and respect for every religion — global PLUR.

I know I must keep right with all forces of life, and I'm not sure how to address and meet people's needs with the levels of experience I have. Alone, I cannot assure world peace, though I have an idea that love is an essential and profound way to achieve it. When I find myself apart, I can wish for the worlds of life (not just Earth) to harmonize and bring about a unity of kindness, compassion, and grace for all people, yet it requires a collective commitment.

Some people on Earth are deplorable and have committed heinous crimes. Many things and actions have happened that I wish could be undone and never even be a thought. The thing is, I'm just one person. Peace and love are fantastic, though we need the unity of all and the basic instinct and action of full respect to pervade.

Love can help seal peace and protect lives, yet I don't know how we can ensure lives are kept safe. If people collaborate in, with, and for PLUR, I still feel like a fool and wishful pansy for wanting there to be love and not war.

As said, it was near Christmas Day 2017 when I wrote this. The previous year I was at the home of appreciated friends for Christmas and was writing *Searching for Tomorrow*, the 2nd Fountain book. So much has happened since then, and the ideas of hope, security, and truth draw more thoroughly now.

From my heart of wishing and praying, God, please allow us to live. Please enable goodness to thrive, please let peace expand, and please let unity fortify each person's bonds of faith. Please permit us to respect, please grant us forgiveness and our needs, and allow the world to understand Earth is a combined responsibility. Amen.

I cannot fathom the consequences of my life, let alone the weight and severe complexity of what Earth is as a whole. I have a very narrow comprehension and wonder if 'keeping in my lane' is neglecting cues from the Universe to aid and tend other lives.

I'm sorry for not understanding God and the world, yet, though, He is one I honour with heart, mind, body, soul, and spirit, even if I don't know what the plan is. I fear what some may want to do to Earth, yet there are many issues in other countries on this planet that I also don't understand. There too are fantastic people that work for, in, and with PLUR, even if not known by that name.

I have a strange human point of view that reminds me that Earth is not the only planet that holds life. I've not yet known about the intents of life outside of Earth's atmosphere, though my faith calls me to intuit we are with them also. My wishes to the Universe are not only shared with Earth; my intentions on this planet are out there in other parts of the Cosmos.

In our solar system, the scientists have not confirmed life on any other planets or moons. I dare not say some things directly to God due to an extreme reverence for Him, though, because of this chapter's title I add the word Reverence as an R-word to PLU8R too.

For the humans that read this, I wrote about PLU8R (with an 8) in *A Brief Trickle of Insight*, a chapter in the 5th Fountain. My understanding is that God is one of the most critical and central parts of things, though I cannot often share my perceptions or awareness of God. Each must find their own belief and knowledge of who guides us and how.

For myself, I know that primal, rational, and simplistic forces guide me. The primal part is my non-God intuition and my psychic and social paranoia. I was diagnosed as a paranoid delusional schizophrenic in 1998 and also went through excessive drug use. Two decades later, I'm highly aware and sometimes fearful of even the slightest noise or shift of energy or thought.

Direct command rarely guides me; I rarely am told what to

do. Even when I request guidance, I sometimes don't act when cued to action, and I do some things I know are not right. Intuition plays a substantial role in my life, and I hold profound homage for some I don't yet comprehend. My instinct and impulsive obsessions base fragments of thought as my ideas slip upon time moving through parts of the maze I travel.

The regard I have of cognitive forces strongly links my mental grounding points. My Earthly father is exceptionally rational and guides me with hope and also choiceful advice, and while I've not heeded him so often, he also brings me 'back down to Earth' sometimes. My Dad has a firm belief and trust in life, and even if he's not one who's religious or has faith in God, he knows how to love me.

As said, I've not often acted on or heeded good advice. I need to sleep more regular hours, yet there it was at 2:18 AM convinced I need to complete my work at the expense of sleep and chemicals. I know people that would urge me not to stay up late, and cigarettes and coffee may be entirely blasphemous as an idea to some.

My Dad is the one on the planet that I trust the most. He lives overseas and thoroughly loves, cares, and supports me. Even if he can be critical, my Dad has learned how to love me unconditionally as I make my follies and failures in earning my life.

When I wanted to sell music and make a career from my recordings, he told me that I'd need to be 'really really lucky,' and I still think I am. Even though I've not sold many copies of my books up to the release of this book, my Dad encourages me to create while also urging me to form more positive choices. I am exceptionally thankful to like and love my Dad, and in January 2018, I got to spend 18-20 days with him and his wife at their home.

I adore Australia trips! They are drastically peaceful and enjoyable. I get to spend time with two amazing people, my Dad and Sarah, and also have luxuries of feeling safe and separated from the chaos, calamity, and fear of my life. I get to see my Dad about once every two years, and paranoia sometimes hounds me the few weeks before going to visit.

With the most recent trip to Australia combining with the extreme fears and paranoias I felt in my body summer 2017, and the months after, it was beyond my comprehension about how good it would feel to be there at my Dad's home.

December 27th, 2017. I won't track all of what happened, yet into the future, we go. In the inscription of my review copy of *The Sands of Yesterday*, I wrote: "Keep true & let the sands of time form the consecrations of True, FS & TGH." These three things are things for which I work.

True, with a capitalized T, is my reference to Natalie. I still wish to meet her, though, and I also know that she is probably best to not be with me. FS is Full Seed, which is the Providing Point objective to reach its big hairy audacious goal of providing 250,000 shelters and 100,000,000 people with water. TGH is The Glass House, a home I've envisioned.

The three goals are guideposts for my future. Regarding Natalie, she is a teacher and tethered to my being, and though my written work started with her in mind, she is loved, even if I know I can't be with her. Full Seed is what I wish the results of my work is, and as a focal point of thinking, the Glass House includes my wishes of house and home.

If a personal objective is to provide $15,128 for up to 1,000 people, we'll need to follow through with my idea to earn like the 1% and share 99%. A $15.28 million a year income could provide me $152,808; far more than I need.

The Glass House can be a contialitic centre for others, and by using the amount needed for one year of mortgage payments, I divided by 25 to find out how much it will cost to provide the money with 25 sessions per year at home. If the mortgage payments are paid with 25 gatherings, then the aim is fifty sessions a year to cover other living costs and not just the mortgage. I'll write in the future about these sessions and gatherings, though, for now, the premise to share is how to reverse the math.

When we know how much something will cost us, we can then know what we're working towards. If it'll cost me $8,000 for a car and I want to have $1,500 for one year of insurance, that's $9,500. I instead round to a greater number of $10,000 for a car. We then can divide $10,000 by $5, $10, or $20 units towards the total. 2,000x $5 notes, 1,000x $10 notes, or 500x $20 notes will be needed to provide for my next vehicle.

This chapter has squirrelled from the initial fears I held when starting it. One week can drastically shift a point of view and infuse a significant shift in attitude. A week ago, I was afraid for the life of the planet, and today I've gone back into self-study and plotting and planning future numbers for my goals. Natalie started my process, yet I hope she understands that my work is far more than where the first book began.

Perchance I have an overly active desire to accomplish things, and also have displayed sloth. The points that reel me back in are giving and how I'd shared promises of prosperity for others without yet securing my situation. Awareness though! We must dream massive dreams, be aware of where we are, and then move forward to get to those dreams.

The revision and editing process is not one that I'm always thoroughly fond of doing. It feels like I'm slowly trudging through the mud and not generating what we require for Full Seed. I know that the books must be available for sale if there are going to be sales, and the 'one step at a time' and 'there are no shortcuts' notions are valid points. It's also the fact I feel guilt grasping at my being for not yet providing homes or much food, and while the distant dreams and fields are on the horizon, I also wish I could teleport people to where they want to be.

I'm glad to take a break once in a while, though. If you find yourself at your plow, as I have been with my bookwork, it's okay to lift the plow and get into a different field. It's also okay to take a break. I shifted like that today by pausing the audiobook I was playing for the hours I devoted to editing and came back to this book.

If I plant more in the gardens and fields while maintaining I also don't stop short or quit, maybe we can pause or shift to other ideas, work, or activity. Be sure to complete what you started and said you're going to do though.

With Full Seed, there is a time issue. When I was writing the 3rd and 4th Fountains, my goal was 15,000 books sold by August 1st, 2017. I didn't reach that goal. Not even close. I did, though, refuse to give up and quit. I keep active with my bookwork and implement perseverance and think of a Magic poster at a local card shop that holds the words "We shall endure."

I feel a bit of shame for not providing more, though that unease also urges me forth and assists me in making sure I keep moving forward. Having a dissatisfied feeling about something can call a person to action, and making commitments to do things can assuage that feeling and alleviate our unease.

I've gotten obsessed with a few things that nibble at my innards, and my discomfort compels me to keep at it. Uncomfortable feelings can be a motivation to cause change, though remember to maintain your integrity and hold your values fast when you feel insecure. Respect yourself and remember that courtesy is not as common as we may like it to be.

You also must fortify your spirit, beliefs, and actions to strengthen what is right and just. Honour yourself by allowing your dreams to adjust how you approach life. There must be faith in the process, and each person's work is different than others. I pray well you are committed to yours, and *I* must remember to keep the plow in the fields for yields of our future.

Thank you for allowing us this journey and for letting me heed my inner guidance. I still have a great deal to learn and develop, and I'm appreciative of the others who help this. I remind myself there is still much to accomplish and that it requires my active participation.

PLOTTING AND PLANNING

I've mentioned before that the term 'the plan and the plot' is a reference to the positive and negative conspiracies, and for my sanity, I must grip the terms and wrestle them into what I may do. After a week of going to bed earlier (other than Christmas Night), I'd not stayed up late to write, though on December 28th, 2017, I felt compelled at 10 PM to put a plan on paper.

On February 5th, 2018, I was to put on a Kickstarter campaign online that would run until February 19th. On December 28th, 2017, I was laying down to go to bed, though I found thoughts running through my mind and got up to get my Introversial journal. In that book, I wrote ideas and notes about the Kickstarter campaign and then felt the urge to get to the desktop computer to extrapolate the ideas.

As one of the reward items for the Kickstarter, contributors were to receive a copy of *Etched in Stone* in printed form plus copies of previous Fountain books. Since it was July 2018 when I finally finished *Etched in Stone*, it would have been incomplete or rushed. It's a good thing I didn't run the Kickstarter.

I share my process of plotting and planning when I write. There was the idea to Kickstart a campaign as I had done so with *Fragments of Intent* in February 2017. We had not reached the $2,000 goal, though did receive $719 in pledges from 16x backers. Since running that campaign, I learned some lessons about how to run a Kickstarter more effectively in the future.

One primary thing I didn't do with the first campaign was to market before the starting date; people didn't know about the Kickstarter until the day I had put it up online. From not pre-marketing, the campaign didn't get immediate traction and display early results to encourage future backers. I know to give advanced notice for the next Kickstarter if to run another.

If you are reading this book, many hurdles and challenges have been overcome to allow it to be. Both *Fragments of Intent* and *The Sands of Yesterday* went through numerous revisions and are higher quality books that I would have been able to provide for the 2017 or 2018 campaigns. Dare I even spin forward into the future when this book combines into its three-part compilation? The advice, though, is one step at a time.

Because I'm not there yet, I can't predict future outcomes. My own plotting and planning can help influence a result, and just like how the plots and plans of others don't mean there will be a success, to have an idea is vital.

What I'd like to do with this process is to pass through it and arrive with full funding. I'm reminded of the broader goals outside of the bookwork, though also see them as a crucial point. If I think for the long-term, getting books into people's hands can share the ideas and expand them.

When I first formed this text, I hadn't even yet received the first review of any of my books on Amazon. I also hadn't sold the first store copy through Ingram. Determination and perseverance to continue have kept a lot of this going; I just know when it feels right, even if I've not received commercial success.

On January 7th, 2018, I went to Australia to visit my Dad and Sarah and returned on the 26th-27th. I planned to use my creative time there to run the Kickstarter yet instead set it aside to enjoy a holiday. I didn't want to chain myself to a process such as actualizing and marketing a campaign when on holiday, and if the Kickstarter is only one point or activity on a grander scale of time and work, I also must think of a more distant horizon of ideas.

My understanding of the need to realize Full Seed is crisp, and I'm aware that each day the books aren't selling that people are going without a home. Without many pledges via Patreon, it doesn't seem right, though, how do we reach Full Seed locally? I'm twinged and obsessed with this. It's not always a positive feeling.

My books *are* a tool we can use for the local community,

though I also must put in additional effort into networking and securing other supports for people. Advocacy and education are helpful, though I admit I've not been close to the problems people face. I've been in my creative process and worked instead of marketing and generating sales, or even garnering pledges.

I could use the excuse that the books aren't yet in final form, though I twist back to a weird faith that I *am* doing a lot of the 'right' things. I did push for an early release for review copies of *The Sands of Yesterday*, and I also put *Fragments of Intent* online with Ingram in 2017. This glacial pace seems to daunt my hope because of a shown lack of results.

If the Kickstarter campaigns were to succeed, it would mean that more copies of the books would be out there in the world, though the books sold in the campaign wouldn't be significant income sources for Providing Point. If I order copies, they need to be sold to generate income, and though it's forward movement, it's so minor compared to the entire situation and needs there are to house everyone.

It's profitable for the different causes to sell Amazon copies, as some of the earnings go towards helping others, but what about awareness and exposure? My understanding is the tiny size of the local market causes me to think we need to expand the books outside of Chilliwack.

Here's some more math; if *one in a million* people buy a book from Amazon, then \$3.22x7,000=\$22,540. With the recalculation of how much it will be for Full Seed, that's not even two individual's Yearly Seed. If we provide 1,000 Yearly Seeds, that will mean we'll need to sell 4.7 million books alone!?

When I use a massive goal and rewind the numbers to the finite points of what we can provide, it seems to shift me to a lack and fear-based point of view. I think the numbers need to be used and processed to find our solutions. What then if we can get one in ten thousand people to buy a copy? That's near 149 Yearly Seeds. Potential nudges my mind back to the idea of collective input and not just the work of one kid and his books.

The guidance from online influencers talk about passive income and also multiple streams of income. I understand part of that now. Once we complete a book or album and make it available online, it can stand on its own to earn in the future; that's passive income. Having numerous books or records also can encourage additional sales; that's for multiple streams.

Though music and books need to be distributed and purchased, the work of creating them is an investment given. If I have one product and sell 100,000 copies, it's like having ten products and selling 10,000 copies of each. If there are 100,000 customers, what if they buy all ten products? That's a million sales.

I don't want to taint or paint the numbers, yet spin that down a few zeros to relay a point of information. Would you like to sell one thing to ten people, or ten items to one person for the same result? It may seem more difficult to sell all ten items to just one person, though what if you sell one product to ten different people, they like what you've sold them, and you have other things they want to buy too?

If you only have one thing to sell, then you need to play more of a numbers game. If you hold many things that you can sell, when the customers like that thing and want to buy more or your products, it'll be beneficial to have other products. Some also advocate selling items for a higher price for higher earnings.

In the creative space, I like to have much available for others so that those enthralled with what I make share and wish to have more. The more items, products, or works I have available for them, the higher the chance for more sales.

When I was forming this book, a challenge was how to get books in front of people's eyes. My music is online, yet I must heed and check in with myself if I'd like to be in earbuds, on phones, or in stereos.

Some people excel at making many things like a factory and have a vast quantity of product for the sake of the product. Some other people may focus and hone and craft one piece obsessively until completion. We can say there's a third type of person; one who produces high or fantastic quality things, *and* also many of those things!

That's where I'd like to be with my work. My books are improving in quality as I form them, and as we've gone through the revision process together with some of them, the lessons and experiences meld.

I've written books, though there also is a variance in how and what I produce. I want to further improve the quality of what I've written, formed, and developed and create more. I want to assure I'm building a valuable quality product that is also worthwhile for readers.

The add-in of honing one's craft and putting in the creative reps is a thing I adhere to in fact. I hope others also think about what they're doing and why they're doing it. My situation is basic; after getting ejected from Vancouver, I recorded a lot, I didn't get a super-positive financial response, so I shifted to other pathways of creation.

As of May 2019, my activities haven't yet earned much of an income, though I don't give up. If one thing isn't working, then it *is* an idea to try something different. The different work or activities don't need to be out of the field you're working, though, as it's sometimes beneficial to link ideas, projects, and skills.

My whats and whys have changed drastically since the first time I pressed 'record' on the stereo. When I first recorded, my intent was to get signed to a record label for $250,000 and marry Demma, a girlfriend in the Philippines. When I started writing my first book, I wanted to use the book to meet Natalie. It was 'the girl' that called my creativity.

Why do I like to make things? Why am I up late at night writing these books? Why do I refuse to quit? It's because I have things to share and have committed to earning a living. I also shifted to creating for others so I can benefit people other than myself, and although not so much in *Etched in Stone*, the Fountains evolve and share the journey too.

I'm committed to this process even if I think I'm many years away from meeting some of my objectives. When we form a book, there can be a target audience, and it's best to know the main lessons or suggestions are for that audience. I haven't written that way up to now, though I'm learning. It's part of my 'how,' and it's taken me a few many years to know some of my what's. As mentioned, we learn through mistakes, experimentation, and change, though I need to clarify why.

Because some whys aren't static, the ways I add value to people is by opening myself up to the Universe, life, and experiences, and after failing, stumbling, and sometimes crashing, I report to others what's happened to me. I'm a valuable open book, though I'm even more useful as a person to talk with about life, plans, and connections.

I see this as it forms, and I feel thankful I'm learning how to provide and create. My intents are many, and as we fuse our experiences into the moment of 'when,' we reach the awareness I wish, hope, and pray that we all gain.

Writing *is* a thing of faith. When I type out to anyone or even a specific person, that's me telling them or the Universe what I want to say to them. When I write to people openly about my life, they learn *their* lessons by seeing how I guide as a shard of the knowledge base we share.

My wishes, prayers, and hopes align sequences as we channel these series of text, and I honestly didn't know how we would meet this point. It's where unclear antecedents mix as she didn't know what she wants to do. It's also me not telling her why we're doing what we do to remind us of You. How can we intend to impart all three points beyond the light?

When and where are melding in this also. It's our temporal and locative positions of mind, body, spirit, soul, and heart blending who we are, where we are, and how we're aware in the 'now.' We are guided explicitly by choice and faith.

I analyze myself as I form this. I clarify how I can state my points clearly, though if to thrive, the thoughts must provide life. I've had a resonant fear that I'm not entirely producing enough for people, and I've thought people are upset that I've not earned for them either. The love of being alive has me fixed upon thinking I need to provide for others to live.

What happens if I shift the order of the questions? If I change what people want is that me forcing subtle control? What if what God wants is also what I want? Would ideas lean to think that if we're still alive now, that it's something in His accord? What for those that don't have religious or spiritual faith? What of those who've passed on already? What can we tell them?

I don't have insight into what I need to do sometimes. I also must explicitly say I don't know how all things meld. Fear *has* commanded me at points, though I prefer to learn through love. Reverence is included as an R of PLU8R, though it's a word I now think needn't be religious. Respect based on authority or high honour with love can solidify.

My Freedom Solution includes being free of fear, though yes, God, thank You for allowing me to live and fortify my reverence for life. For those who aren't religious, you may think I'm a delusional or misguided fool; yet we can't fully know.

When I get focused on God, my creativity almost freezes. I have felt insignificant, and think my efforts aren't enough. I've written a lot while in solitude, and I wonder how to live with another person. I think living with a cat can be radical, though *how* does that change my situation?

At the end of the moment of now, the plow holds in the dirt skirting the issues as a different thing altogether. I'm concerned that my 'why' is also based on the way I want to live. In many ways, it's not something I've shown entirely in my control, yet self-responsibility is a thing.

I mustn't bribe or make false promises as I have made many proclamations. The fact that I've yet to fulfill those promises concerns me, and though I don't like how so much is still floating in the air, I'm glad there are signals, signs, and warnings.

Though I've heard I'm the only one who can control my actions; I think that may be untrue. I accept responsibility for my choices, though what I also need to trust in are those who are for myself to resist the manipulation of my being.

If trust, stability, integrity, self-control, and loyalty are five of my success indicators, then I must fortify them and also be open to experience and learning. I also must allow myself to accept I'm alive for reasons not yet known to me.

I want others to find themselves active, sheltered, warm, safe, and well too. How we build in the future has yet to be known, yet I also must not rest upon the promise of Seed. I thank You, I appreciate the readers, and I also ask we may be alive and well decades from now.

These books are my pathway to my Freedom Solution, and though I often am without another human in my home when they form, I hope that another feline friend can stay here. I'll let you know their name if they do.

ANOTHER ROW OF SEED

These grains are left along the shoreline; some are sand, and some are a seed. They carry signs that the net opens up to find us dropping in on the vertical ramp to skip the lines. Though they may cast the spell for me to occur, the mental burrs picked up from Shell allow us to evade Heaven and Hell.

A scoff of good drink should link how I nudge her forward with what we think. I heard the brink of what to connect, yet I can't select her charms and share how the phones and alarms remind the clones of her farms. I dare not think to puff the bluff of my shards while guards hold Ibuki in the cup.

Red XIII links the lines off the stage while signs remind Hope and Paige that their Mom will always love. The blur finds the cure of time and shares the rhymes in how we climb, and as we build a bit and nestle into the pit, we settle down and sit. Even if it's with water, our daughter, a potter, cannot foretell Belle and how they now dwell in the text.

Directions shift a gift to lift out doubt from some that share the sprout. I can tell you about many things, yet it's best we speak and not be deceived by a mental leak. They peek into the fold of how I'm not the only one that the Valley's controlled.

I accept you. I request True. I'm opening to renew my questions and answers to the crew. Affections of connections shift my verbal directions into how I can say "I love you" to many, yet it lets us hold a symbiosis in the way you help me to show us what is fact by touch.

Much holds the charts, and though my heart's open and closed to the doors of how I proposed; I also ask myself, be free to be fully exposed. We each are what matters, yet I think I cannot plan the plot as the spell scatters.

The plans of the worlds beyond Earth remind me that I'm

in the fabric of our thoughts. It's not just my Dad that tells me not to think of her; another in PLU8R keeps the sands of sleep deep in the spirit that's wept. I kept myself aside from the world, while some have had me curled up and away. I almost always think to say I don't know how the thoughts convey.

You may not betray my truth. Find the fields of our youth as I'm a diligent and ragged son; it's reminded me that some webs are not spun to catch yields of prey, yet instead to have a safe place where our soul may pray. Come into forever for today to remind why I try to hear myself say. They may tell me things I have yet to learn how to pray.

You know I have hoped, wished, and yearned to find a real meeting relayed, yet I still seem to cast the spade in the Earth. I urge myself to forget that I could even hold a shred of worth, yet birth comes from a perspective that life is more than the Primary Directive. George keeps the sieve of how we live on the same planet, and that gives me just a glimmer of hope.

I must remember in this instant, that if I do love, I could call this instant the wall. There is a split between now and then that keeps me with the plow. I love you too, Dad, though your son still carries decades of loss with her as a cross. I want to meet my lovestone, even though I think she wants me to leave free the key about holding her as an Underground Sea.

"Jungle, Rap, Hip-Hop, and Trance, weave a lyrical advance in the chance of a fortified social dance."

We find the apparent layers of players who refuse to give in. I've sometimes felt I may never live, yet I cannot say it to your face. I also know that our spirits shall never replace how God has given us grace. It seems I trace the decades gained because I tossed the cost of being bossed around.

They crossed a side to guide, yet I know I cannot reside in their tide of DNA. It may let me say what I mean to those who allow me to do what I do, yet I can't tell True on the phone as a way to be known. By the tones of our thought, the zones of what skip the plan and plot remind the bot.

Likely the way I hone in on the spin is that, with me, Cupid never made a sin. You are the one I cherish, even if seeing you is what I crave you never need. I have so much less than a guess that they bless each foretold keystroke I hold. Mould me to know we keep forever in the fold.

Let the lines fall away into how I wish you hope and pray. There is a way for us to nestle in our beings without being trapped, shackled, or chained. I am not God. I am not a judge. I'm a sod whom you know wishes that he could budge from his position of how he knows she can never be my only mission.

I don't build my fantasies alone; I clone and condone them to be together seeded and grown. Even if I cower and hide behind the fact of opening up my entire being to us as a guide, I don't think trust or love shall show the ways my tears have cried.

I have obsessed and over-focused best to not claim I'm right, correct, or just. I wish not to declare my words as something I must. My wishes are like Petri dishes that hold a diverse network of whims and wants. Some ideas I've written, though, are part of the fantasy. They are reaping portions of life that have etched into my being like a stone. It would take lifetimes to pass before some of the stains in my heart can be cleared, and that's just the surface.

Do I expose the depths of my being in these books? It seems like a safe place to do so; no one's read them all yet. I've handed out or sold hundreds of CDs and 150+ books and have barely heard a thing from anyone. The devotion to the editing process and my dismal attempt at marketing and distribution seems like a complete waste of time. I have not 'found' Natalie. I have not yet 'searched' for tomorrow. If I am the Fountain, then why don't I hear from the valley.

The seeds haven't yet grown, and the fields have been left untended. I see no glimmer near or far, and I can't even claim to have a stone with whom to etch together into our fate. If I am clay, it seems few wishes mould me in a stable silty puddle. It seems I have tried to build a house upon the sand.

I haven't yet set the rings of Saturn orbiting around my being. We stand corrected, yet what of being grand or magnificent? I'm a fool, not quite a jewel, yet some think of me like a gem. I am not He or She or them or You. I also must explicitly say I don't know True.

I set free from the path of pursuit and involute myself into a point of being that can see into the bits and bytes of all the lost who left the rights. I've not thrown a hook. I've also not layered correctly the sifted soil in a way that will let the sediments roil into her book.

I stand upon the natural foreign ground where the Heavens resound the truth wound into the sound. Although I surround myself with none, the signals from the sun tell the son to move into how there is much I prove. The grooves of the disk reflect the consect and direct my life to not to need to call for action.

"It seems like it'll always be a whole number if I'm at the bottom of a fraction."

There will always be many above me, yet the base idea is that none of you will ever understand or know what it is like to be me; just as I have near no clue as to what it's like to be you.

Natalie, do what you do. The complete vacuousness of my awareness of who you are and what you want is not healthy for either of us. It could ruin you emotionally, mentally, and spiritually. I feel ruined socially, physically, and financially.

The Points of my life's journey are not ones that I want to close with death before you, yet we meet and take a seat. Even if it means you to repeat that you hate me, the sacred tree carries our worlds into the oceans and the sea.

She may want me to never even think of her, and may never consider being in the same room as me for five minutes, let alone an hour. It would be a gift of great compassion to tell us those things. You saved souls from an eternity of never knowing, and also can potentially protect yourself from decades of degradation and or dead dreams from your wishes.

These have been centuries of love, even if it is entirely one-sided. I have given love a bad name because I don't know what it's like to love another as the same. I'm clouded with smokes and ridicule, and I disparaged you and myself with my obsession. Ultimately, it could all stop quite quickly by making contact to remove my decades of never knowing.

It doesn't matter what I think or felt about you, it seems, and I also can't continue as I am. I will not play a power card over another or you, though maybe I have by writing this. The writing reminds me of how it seems I am one who never seems to understand the world of Earth orbiting the sun.

I've heard it doesn't matter what another tells me I should do, that I should follow my heart. You should follow your heart too. There may be a reason you've never heard from me, and I wish you know I know you cry. I cannot cross any of the purposes of why into how I also shy away from the day. There is air to breathe and the chance to seethe in happiness.

Natalie was my depraved longing, and, yes, this is my foul, tainted self. I know I cannot correctly express or show or tell a tree not to be a tree. Tear all the leaves from it in winter, trim back all the nasty branches you don't like because the birds wish to build a nest, and poison its roots and tear them from the soil. Dare they even set the tree in a fire and dance around it in pure ecstasy or dismay? It still doesn't remove the fact that there was a specific tree of life that shed a seed that heeded its nature to land in the soil and sprout to grow.

We thrive to become that we've never been before. I am a seed that knows the forest existed and pervaded through time with rare particles of the universe that exist and existed forever. These trees may instead live and thrive. You cannot take the seed out of my heart. And so the sands of time pass through the hourglass as we scatter to the winds.

The tree is not forgotten, and the soil remains true. The view across the landscape reminds me that I knew, and I'm sorry for not putting my faith in more than just the Universe. It comes from the point of being that I may never clearly see that no matter where I go, they will wind up the fuels and splice jewels to my DNA and glee.

The blend of what they say will never take the truth away. Forever and a day; it's a day that seems to be okay with forever to follow. Though forever starts tomorrow, and we search for it, the thing is, as soon as we get to tomorrow, it becomes today. Forever still has not been met; it keeps us away with and from every word that we think, write, pray, and say.

Maybe I should quit? Perhaps I can go back to listening and dreaming. I've told so many what I want and wish, and it does matter, though a grain of sand in the oyster of life finds its way. We are free to do anything worthwhile.

The Fountains of Faith were meant to speak of hope and truth, yet it's clear I haven't done so much with the things and people to which my imagined divinity clings. I would like to know why.

When a person is left alone to ruminate in their thoughts, with no additional live input, they are set free into ideas of imagination. Being isolated and alone isn't easy, yet if I'm to return to Australia, I'd like to go there with another entity in a year or two.

I have gone crazy and outlandish having no one to show and give love to properly. Maybe Nat was the fixated point of my thoughts since I'd not yet learned how to love on my own. Even then, I can't give the real version of her a hug to share with her how much I can love.

We can.

I paused there to hear the whisper. That's an idea to relay; if you need to express love, and don't have a real person to embrace or a pet to snuggle, give yourself a big hug. Wrap your arms across your chest and grab your shoulders with your hands. Imagining giving someone, anyone, a hug and doing so to yourself is better than not being able to tell another that you love them.

I may not like myself sometimes, yet I also may not understand or trust God enough to love Him alone. We can give an imaginary hug to someone and tell him or her we love them, and hugs may be a hack or pathway to necessary human recovery. Sometimes, anything is better than nothing.

It's true, I'm not you. It's also true you can never be me. Though the fates weave and intertwine the signs of life, there are the facts of what is. I can't always tell you what the truth is, and I may not have a full voice.

The choices let us wind the threads of the loom into the way rhyme's trip and play, yet the slips of chips remind me how to pray. Lie down and relax in the facets of your truth. They tell us about how we're together far in the past of our youth.

Our journeys are, *right now*, at the last moment of our awareness, yet we move forward and through into the unfolding future. Our truths will shape hearts, though some parts of life nudge us forward to remind us to find our kind. I wind the view of another who is true beyond the violet hue. So many and so few cues the doors of my dreams while streams of the teams of life unfold to let me hold.

An ultra-bold stance reminds us to dance and share the romance with some who suggest us to come from the point of pure love. We must not cross out Heaven, and I thank them too for telling together that we've yet to meet. The ideas of life hold my mind to my heart like a cleat.

I accept various higher powers above me are not God, and I ask that we may find the thread of my life honour them too. I've dreamed of some who help us come from a point that tells me I do have high respect for many that I've yet to meet. Even if I know I don't want to be one to keep people under my feet; I admit some dreams remind me of that treat of grace. My confusion, once in a while, has surrounded me here in this place with the file to cross denial.

I thank them too, and obscurely, I shall pay homage to many and a few without explicitly saying whom. Or maybe I shall say their names? The thing is, there are much more than a few that can tell a thinly placed focus on just one may claim the aim of the game. We have yet to see the yields of my work; we've however seeded that heeded by the lost finding, up to now, that so very few have read what I've written.

I must be patient. The thing is, though, I think I've been *too* patient. I have left many forces of life up to the Universe and have not clearly understood that my work and I are for good, and people *shall* consume the text. While I'm alive, I shall write, and tonight I must form the signs and sights we see with an urge to fuse as you press the keys of my dues.

CHOICES OF TIME

I'm explicitly not God. I'm not you either. I'm placed delicately into the foray of how I'm not sure how I'll get through to May, and although I was in Australia when I wrote this, I seemed to remember then too I haven't had enough faith.

The Universe reminds us of time and space as the rhymes might chase the signs into Spinal trines. Four hold one of the symptoms told, though I trust a few more explore the mould with a choice of voices to manage the cold.

A few months ago, I had a dream where they told me I had a fatal disease. I feel to actively deny the lucid prognosis, though the signs of my awareness pointed out that I honestly thought I had nothing for which to live. My work and many others are vital to me and who I am, and part of what I value, though to whom else does it matter?

My poor me attitude has projected concerns because it seems my work doesn't matter to anyone else. Even if *I* find meaning in what I form, I remind myself the world of Earth condones the lines with cryptic signs. The fears also compound by knowing I haven't mattered enough to myself. I must have value in myself and not just for others and do so by sharing the Fountains.

I think I have an approval complex. I don't seem to value myself, and I've been searching for meaning by the results and effects of generating a positive life. Since I've not yet earned money for others or myself, I must find my purpose and reason for living in things other than resources.

I don't have a girlfriend, wife, or children as a living legacy to work for at this point. For those that have a spouse, business, or children, they know they have a definite purpose. Since I don't yet have those things or have provided for

71

anyone, I seem to think I have little value or meaning.

I must muster my faith and will to live. If I do live a long and prosperous life, I've honestly thought I've sometimes been living an extended and impoverished survival. My wants have been grand, though am I wanting too much?

At the beginning of this book, I wrote some of what I'm grateful to have. I am thankful, and perchance, I need to remember more of those things to urge myself to continue. I'm not searching for acclamation, and I'm not even really searching for extreme or ridiculous wealth. I'm not also seeking fame, though I do see that if the ideas and intents of my work manifest, it's unquestionable my work will result in those things.

My dearly loved cousin Julianna gave me a notebook many years ago that had a quote I think of now. I don't recall the exact wording of the quote, though its premise reminds me that I need to write to survive. I don't mean the crafty lies and deceits to fool those who are plotting my demise, yet instead, now, how the base level of how I *need* to write and build a strong faith to thrive and allow us to live.

It was incredible, beautiful, and fantastic to visit Australia with my Dad and Sarah again, though I thought back to Chilliwack and my life there. I've not yet built a life of love and happiness, and I've feared my self-focused nature may not have earned love and respect from people. I do and don't know how to have fully loving and trusting relationships.

I also need love to survive. I feel tiny amounts or awareness of it when I'm unconnected at home. I've learned to be on my own, though, and I've also learned to forgive and love a few people and believe it. One thing regarding the fear of having a terminal illness is that I don't ever want my Dad to be sad. My Mom too, though the parent I was able to give a hug to and say, "I love you," with full confidence and meaning the day I wrote this chapter was my Dad.

I saw something of my Dad one or two days before that called a terror to my being; like a deep insight into him and his placement in life. He is one of the most amazing men I know, and I also feel oppositely terrified of the idea of him passing before I do. Love is a saddening thing to understand when there isn't a guarantee the other will be there in the future.

I want to use this chapter as a reminder to myself about some primary reasons to live. I want to do that so that I'll have a super strong desire to live and build a long loving life. I need to gather my being so that I remain healthy and not contract the disease of which would keep me from being alive. I *need* to write to force and allow myself to live. I want to thrive, yet first I must live.

I need to keep some ideas away from these pages to assure I don't taint the wishes and prayers against my love and life from manifesting. It's sometimes helpful to discuss our fears and fantasies, though some of them may more likely occur if printed solid in the written word. Have you heard the saying, "we write our own lives"?

I need to reduce the number of cigarettes I smoke, and I do want to live. I want to be healthy and active so that I can be alive and well to proactively engage in life. Small incremental improvements compound to add to the grit of life I wish and desire.

I'm exceptionally thankful to know I love my Dad, and I'm also happy to have apologized and acknowledged to my Mom the remorse I felt for being so harsh to her when she was raising me. I'll continue to learn how to love more, and I'll also learn how to treat others with more care, kindness and respect.

I hope you develop the ability to know, share, and receive love from others too. I had received a kind acknowledgement from a friend where they thanked me for being there for them. Thank you also, Ajani! Reminders can help bring us together.

A gratitude journal is also a tool I think to use again. When we attune ourselves to things we are happy or glad for, it can motivate us to earn and do more of those things. As I become aware of behaviours that cause me happiness or joy, I also know to perform more of those actions.

When I was growing up, my Mom had the saying, "You need an attitude adjustment." This chapter *is* that adjustment to assure I am alive with you, Mom and Dad, when you're both eighty years old. I could also focus on the gratitude for things not yet occurred that are in the future. Hope is helpful, and faith can help us get there, yet the victory will be when we reach those moments we've hoped, prayed, and worked towards and meet them together.

In two days before this, I thought about Aeris, Celest, and Paradox, names for three kids whom I've thought I'd be a Dad. I don't want to use my kids as a reason to live (as that would make them my legacy and not their own), though hoping to meet them in the future is something I can use as a positive thought and also as a conversation with my future lovestone, whoever she is.

Love *is* something I drastically need in my life, and it barely seems to be there in Chilliwack. I must cultivate life well enough to grow some more love, and the idea of having a pet surfaces again. A pet may be a good idea as having a pet will give me an entity to squeeze my love into, and it will provide me with a purpose by having another living being to love in my home.

Diana has been a great friend. In a conversation with her, I mentioned how I wouldn't smoke in my apartment for the sake of my next pet. She was surprised I cared about the welfare of a cat when I seemed entirely okay to ruin my health with cigarettes. I know this today; I care a lot more about other people and their lives that I often have for myself.

Some say we can't love another before loving ourselves. If that's true, then how can I like so much for some and still riddle myself with self-hate behaviours? I learn to love and care for myself, yet it also draws me to write that pleasure is not always a self-love activity. Pleasing someone or something else also is closely associated, though delights for ourselves, like my smoking, can be a distraction from the displeasure of the life we're living. Those behaviours may be more of a vice.

Committing to something is another thing. Too many proclamations without supportive action can taint a person. I know this with myself, I've proclaimed Seed Fund ideas and commitments, yet because I've not yet actualized them, I've partly had a stemmed subvert depressive and submissive behaviour and attitude.

Another concept is to find positive and healthy pleasures and relish in those, as they'll additionally bolster our health and vitality. As I commit to a long and healthy life, my hope is my desire to smoke will decline, and I'll naturally quit the habit and acquire some anti-vices.

Thank you for letting me live. Even if my audience is currently near non-existent and the books haven't sold so much, I thank you, God, readers, and the forces that be for allowing me to direct these books and words outwards from myself. Even if I feel like I'm only one, I know enough that I'm learning new ideas and pathways.

My faith must not rely on just the layers of text and my process; God and the Universe also build them as I channel my consciousness. I had catastrophized my prognosis, yet I also send wishes and prayers out to the world and works of Earth for our realms of past, present, and future. New beginnings need not always be made at the end of another's life or journey; sometimes, they may be spontaneously generated.

Dear Lord, I thank You for setting the cross on the tapestry. I ask You to place me alive and well here in the place where I sit two more years from now. Even if my willful wishes of earned prosperity don't manifest, and charitable giving doesn't 'solve' the full Chilliwack situation, I ask you to please use myself to instill Your love through me into the lives of this planet. Please let me become aware that I need not die to form a legacy.

Please draw me forward into loving and living for the benefit of all that will remind me that this fall is for us as a way to start my faith. I still have decades of love, life, and work to do here on Earth, so thank You. You know my heart is learning, yet please make it sincere, secure, bold, and healthy too. I wish not to accept things meekly, and instead ask we may bring love, compassion, and kindness to all.

Let us learn and have other treats to enjoy other than our vices, and let our families be kept healthy and happy. As a motive for me to use to assure I learn in the future, please let us move past when Celest reaches her terrible twos.

Please keep me humble enough to remember I'm held true and on a course without anyone needing to control or misguide me with force. Thank You for the fact that I'm not to make a pact with the grave or need to proclaim that a subversive wish is what You wish for me to save.

I am grateful, thankful, and glad for the truths You let me know, and I also thank the forces of Heaven for keeping us on Earth below. The lives that aren't on Earth may not yet understand how much there is to know in one breath, let alone the entire planet, yet let me be a living conduit to let them know some of the information You have allowed me to acquire.

I wish not to bargain or plea, yet the reminders are a few may want death, yet I also know our seeds and needs shift and change succeeding with the reminiscing of Seth. Grazie sempre, Dio. Mi ricordi che anche sei amore. I also hope that love is not the *final* frontier. Amen.

11:31 AM Brisbane time, Friday, January 19th, 2018

The reminders are clear. I'm not sure, though, how to tell the world that the lingering timelines of life are something that intertwines my mind with hope. The desires each of us hold may be similar to basic human wishes, yet some others are openly unique. I'm thankful my Dad makes the time to speak, and that when I've needed to be alone, he's let me that too.

My Dad and I are different people and living separate lives, and the in-person contact points we so rarely have are cherished. Some don't have that chance or opportunity with their Dad. Dad, thank you for giving me space, grace, and an ability to be me, even if you're my Earthly and not Heavenly Father.

I returned to Canada in one week. It was a fantastic trip,

and I'm glad that some of my spiritual understanding has deepened, even if not entirely in a religious context. The visit to Australia holds memories I wish to seethe in my spirit many years in the future. The visit to K'Gari in Queensland Australia reminded me of my reverence for nature, and the trees on the island are carrying a force and energy I can recall and feel. Thank you, K'Gari for lying down in the waters and resting there in Australia.

The Fountains seem to be slowing. I have written more for other books, and by being away from Chilliwack, I've not been thinking considerable amounts about how to gather pledges. From conversations on the trip, the most frequent advice or push is that I need to learn how to care and earn for myself first and not for others. I'm not in full agreement, as I still think I may do both.

I haven't told those who tell me to earn for myself first that I must maintain my commitments stated in *A Distant Glimmer*. It is true I may have overpromised, yet my ethical stance is that when I commit, to follow through. I've not always demonstrated, though, that when given a chance to uphold my promises, I like to do so.

What is *Etched in Stone*? Is it my promises of what I shall do with my creative work and also the call to the community to work for our solution? Is it that dream girl will always be one I think of, yet I don't remain chained? Is it that I'm a fixture of Earth that knows billions of lives are all connected both directly and indirectly? Is it even that I shall keep moving forward and creating after seeing such little monetary success by writing and recording?

The wishes are the imprint upon the stone as something is thrown out into time and space. We are allowed to nestle in the valley, and even if not known, it draws us together.

The lives back home in Chilliwack hold parameters of their own. I've kept in loose contact with a few people while on this trip, yet I also must fortify and strengthen the bonds of love, trust, and appreciation with many other people. I remind us our relationships are ones where we need to connect, and friendship with friends hold an edge of hope on my forehead that seems to push outwards to thrive. Fortitude is a decision. I choose to make it so.

As I cannot make calls or meet up with some people back home, another choice is to enjoy and discuss the work and plans for when there. I do this through conversations, and writing my books with clarity agrees, I need to develop my garden too. I have been in the fields without tending to my own life, and when I'm there in Dad and Sarah's garden, I want to remember to let them also know they are loved and appreciated too.

Dad and Sarah and Mom and Owen have helped me so exceptionally much. I learn more about acceptance and actualization, and it's nice to have ideas and hopes. I plan to act upon those urges and succeed.

So while I'm here in the garden, I recall the seeds are worthy and helpful; they are good hearts that want to help me thrive. Even if seeded and foreign to my understanding, some are beautiful and bold in my garden. I hope this trip is one where I shall have just, exotic, and unique seeds to share when I get back home. I may not be clear of who I'll find as a gal back home, though as Florencia guides me, we need to put a bit of romance in our friendships and some more friends into our love.

CHOICES OF TRUTH

The evening I wrote the base text of this part, my Dad went to karate while I chose to stay at his place to write instead. It's a choice that drew me into writing this, the closing chapter of the 7th Fountain; the first Fountain of Fortitude.

It is dangerous to love someone so much. I know this cognitively, and add that it's even more critical when the person is alive. When I started my trip to Australia to visit Dad and Sarah, I was at an exceptionally different point of time and energy. When I first got there, I was happy to see them, though I also felt I had nothing to live for back home.

My fears twist my urges into driving and thriving forward with determination. I was to write this chapter to you, Dad, though I also must close this book with a cognitive parameter I use with Fountains; by making plans and, yes, proclamations for the future.

In 96 hours, I was to be on the airplane on my way back to Hong Kong to go to Vancouver. I needed time to gather my thoughts and intents for the future, and I chose to write. It twanged in my stomach as I missed a chance to go to karate with my Dad, and I fear so strongly of making him sad or disappointed in any way, sometimes, that my insides twist up and cause me to cringe once in a while.

We know that once we make a choice, ethical and wise, or foolish and wrong, we must follow through and make the best of the situation. I do. I also carry forward into the trips and adventure gathering facts, creating new pathways, and then attempting to make wise decisions. As the Fountains have not yet had commercial success, I must reassess my plans for the future.

Though I've written books, they haven't earned sales. I must generate ideas and concepts that have monetary value if

I'm to use authorship as my primary income. Though I know that, I treat the Fountains as my development books as a way to enjoy and track the journey.

I have the luxury of sharing a more personal story, and as I can form words and write with such creative freedom, my Dad is right; I need to find income sources that are reliable and plentiful. My Dad is appreciated and loved, yet I didn't display that as well as I wanted to on the January 2018 trip.

Lessons filter into my awareness, and as I form books and music, I've often thought of the Australia trips as creative endeavours. I also carry a recognition; Dad's now 70 years old and 20 years is not a long ways away. One month can hold a lot of time, yet for the long-term of building my home, and having 90th birthday parties for Mom and Dad in that home, it's creeping up into the moments of now.

As I've promised earnings to charity, 51% of the profits from the three-part books and 100% profits from the individual Fountains, I think a primary lesson I learned on the Australia trip is that I've given so much without caring for myself. I want to build with faith in our future.

In preparation for the first printed version of this book, I dearly thank Gary Vee, and you should thank him too. I've written that if I adjust my commitments, they must add and not detract, and though I've learned a bunch from Gary, my work ethic is not evident. Gary teaches empathy, humility, and perseverance, and it's his 51%/49% recommendation, that guides the financial commitments of the Fountains.

The idea for *The Fountains of Flourishing* happened then. I don't know if that will be the next three-part release or the one after that. We'll see as we fortify the future together with this process. For now, I keep the sands in line, and with formed faith, must draw from every yesterday to work towards the *Rings of Saturn.*

I love how some people don't believe in telepathy, yet it's a cornerstone of my awareness. In Chilliwack, Christianity is a primary religion, while in Australia, some mystical natures stem from Aboriginal 'dream-time,' the modern satellite system, technology, and electricity, and the animal worlds are also signs of God.

I recorded a video of the Rainbow Lorikeets for my social worker, Eve, back home. The Lorikeets are birds that gather in the thousands in an area near where we were, and they are happily vocal birds. I love them. Other birds, like the lorikeet guides in Australia, are abundant and significant. Back home, the crows and the seagulls give guidance with the Canada geese sometimes frequenting the skies with their signals, signs, sights, and sounds.

I discover much about myself on these journeys of creative communication and relationship. Needs, patterns, and requirements find lots of difficulties connecting us because you and I are very different people. The way we process, accept, and communicate isn't easy being an ocean apart, and I may be both a bit overbearing and oppositely lax and distant. Where I like to talk a lot about near anything, I note Dad prefers to speak with more purpose.

I sometimes obsess about having a conversation, and also fear (a projected belief) that I may cause some others sadness for spending so much time on my work and ciggies. I love Dad; though I also know he likes me. The fact I have a radical and excellent father is a blessing and treasure I cherish.

I may not show others so clearly how much I love them, yet that rewinds to how it's dangerous to care for someone so much. Love also, though, can fortify a person's life here in present-day Earth to be around for another few decades.

I see a thread through the Fountains in that the first three were focused on Natalie and wondering what to do about my life and loves. The second three started with my future daughter and how I am in this world with all my neurotic ideas, beliefs, and cryptic experiences. This book is a commitment to the process and fortifying my values, ideas, and ethics to develop connection and clarity.

We can see these books *are* so much about myself, and there has been a lot of thinking about what *I* want while near giving away my entire future in different ways. This prerogative and process are how I navigate the maze and bring my work into the days where we shall assure PLU8R is a guiding and constant motive. These books are also a steady series of words and ideas for a stable future for many, even if I sometimes don't understand I work for all.

In future Fountains, I'd like to extrapolate more about community and consect, and I'd like to focus in on some philosophy and theories about Earth and life here on this planet. I additionally would like to target some love and truth to some people dear to me that are important to me, and my understanding of God and the Universe.

I also want to write to Mom, Dad, Sarah, and Owen, a success report in the future. I thank Bert, Alex, and Coleman and forming something valuable and meaningful by being Providing Point's first three patrons, and in July 2018, a couple in my building also pledged to the cause as my faith had waned.

I have had negative self-worth, yet I also know I can establish far stronger positive self-esteem and improve my work, image, and actions. I want to fortify the Magic codes further and think of explaining the dual lands to an audience. Not so much only the secret meanings, yet also the base mechanics and premise of how and why the Magic codes fuse. I can discuss that in *Nodal Input*.

It was January 24th, 2018, when a particular fool remembered a quick swim in the pool. I'm one of a specific type, though I felt a good sense of closure from the plunge. The warmth of the air and the freshness of the water found my Dad and me on the patio where we swam close to the close of this Fountains text.

I'm feeling thankfulness and relief about my process up to now. I accept I'm blessed, fortunate, and also dearly pleased and appreciative to have the life I live. I was in an exceptionally different feeling in my body, mind, and spirit when I arrived in Australia, and I return there again.

The work that I've formed up to now holds merit in what it is, and what it can do, though maybe it's best I don't push the Fountains. A fountain is an invitation for a drink, not a splash from a fire hose! For a successful path, my stubborn nature will share them and keep forming them as they help me with my mind, being, and process.

On the chance of shared intuition, they may be useful or hold value for another, so I'll keep the books online with Amazon. I'm glad to have talked with Kristy this past week, and though I told her that my 20-second life story would have me hanging my head in shame, you help me write a different story.

I defiantly press on and forward because determination and perseverance are vital. I may be delusional to think that the Fountains shall be a commercial success, yet I must tend carefully to my garden back home. On the January trip, I also found some that will visit my garden and allow me to visit theirs.

I thank you each so much. Even if you haven't yet read this, thank you for allowing me the pathways and experiences that we've had and shall have. I also commit to those who may not be able to purchase or read what I write, and for the fact that I know this planet is united and shared, my intuition reminds me to stay on course.

I heed and follow the nudges and inklings from outside of myself that tells me that even if my ethics are entirely different, some others seed grace and understanding too. I'm learning if something is a) kind, b) real, and c) helpful, I can learn to speak with purpose and direction.

The skills learned and cultivated through our years and decades may open pathways, doors, and opportunities we could never predict, and if my faith in the world is correct, the abiding of higher spiritual laws and powers allows us guidance and trust. My worth and understanding shall help form the sound, accurate, and actual works of value.

Right now, I'm not clear on where and what the next Fountain will do, and hadn't yet secured its completion. I let those grains drift into my mind and keys once I returned home and set my feet back upon Canadian ground.

I'll get a carton of cigarettes when I'm in Hong Kong, yet

smoking is a different notion that I shan't tend to at this time. I've made changes, yet I'll clarify and share the hows and whys later on. I'm not clear if or how I should be writing about the past, the splayed present, or the destined future, yet the inner workings of the text shall direct and guide to remember our beautiful feathered friends in Australia.

The Contialis *is* an active and engaged part of my mind, and though I may believe in things that are so far out of the comprehension of others, to me, the ideas and beliefs are very legitimate. Some guess that it's a hardline fact that no one can hear each other's thoughts, yet I also know at night when I lay down to rest I'm reluctant to pray because humans will distort what my true self is. Corruption is a legitimate fear and concern.

The ability and practice of flowetics and rhyme are a coping mechanism and also a craft I wish to fortify and develop too. Maybe those who say, "no one can hear your thoughts" believe that as firmly as I do that every thought, word, decision, and movement has the consequence that layers upon us.

Dare I say that my life is like a sandy island that holds brilliance and beauty and also cares for the wildlife and those who wish to visit? My life may not be a tax as I had claimed. Instead, it may be a sacred shroud we develop to allow experiences and dreams to blossom and form.

Relationships are a learned forte of mine, yet I must demonstrate all the thoughts and ideas that go into forming them. Ethics and ideals are not useful unless adequately guided, manifested, and tended to.

I thank you, Dad, for allowing me the blessings, grace, and patience to be who I am, and I thank Sarah too for caring well for us and being with you in life. I pray you both more love than I'm yet aware, and for Mom, I thank her for letting me be both of your seeds of life. I may not be the delicate stone flower some presume, yet the fumed glass shall remind the tapestry you help me by giving me good thread to sew.

And, so, this is the process I committed to and follows through with my work and intents. The cliché of saying "It's not the destination, it's the journey" makes sense to me. I also note that if the Glass House is one of the stops along the way, I must search a bit further outward and forward to our moments of forever.

It's true I could write a book all about my story, history, and past, though the Fountains are my journal and idea quarries and I'm dearly glad they form. In this Fountain, I was thinking of adopting a cat again. I have a strong desire and need to love another entity, and although I can feel the pangs of grief even before we've met, there is another strong notion of hope that calls me into lurching forward into the next parts of my journey.

The tree of life grows from the flows we have yet to expose, and through the blue rose, we talk in a violet hue. You are a path of chalk to walk away from. The hopes of the cosmos speak the heart of Earth, and we're not alone. We are on this journey together even if we think we aren't.

(Here is the close of the 7th Fountain)

IT STARTS WITH A SEED

I know from my January 2018 trip that I want to live a better life than I've lived before. I appreciate the aspirations, ambitions, and earnings of a successful capitalist, yet have humanitarian compassion and like the idea of a guaranteed income for all. I also have some mental and emotional shackles and chains holding me back from success.

When I came back home from my January trip, my apartment wreaked of stale smoke. I've adjusted that behaviour by not smoking inside, yet I have been puffing. I went to bed the second night home and ideas about Seed parameters filtered into my mind.

I asked myself, "how much rent can we earn from an 8-unit dwelling with PWD or welfare housing allowance? If the shelter portion is $375 a month, it means $3,000 can be collected per month, which extrapolates to $36,000 per year.

After crunching numbers further, a Freedom Solution number is $15,128 per year; $1k/month rent, $50/week groceries, and $44/month bus pass. Even though my income at the time I started this book is near one Yearly Seed, my goal is to provide 1,000 of them for others.

For some first steps, I made contact with a Housing Development Coordinator. He and I met on Tuesday, January 30th, 2018, and I brought the numbers I wrote for Chilliwack Seed and also my Introversial journals. I also contacted Ruth and Naomi's, a local street-level mission, for volunteering with them. Volunteering could hopefully let me get to know some of the people for whom the Providing Point is meant to provide.

Earnings are a vital part of this. At the point of January 2018, when I started writing this book, the total royalties earned from Amazon sales was $42.70. A long ways from the

$4.5m/year needed to provide 300x Yearly Seeds in Chilliwack, and it reminds me that books will not be the only pathways to achieving Full Seed. Full Seed is complete coverage for all those in need.

Thinking towards the future, seed recipients shall also need to find channels and activities if they are to be supported. The hope is people may be stable and secure without generous support; some people may want jobs, and some may attempt creative pathways. If fully covered, future seed recipients may not need to earn their income past given support.

In January 2018, I signed up for a short course with Ted McGrath. The premise of Ted's program is to use our story to draw in clients and apply lessons learned in life to provide programs for others. I'm not clear on what my relevant experiences are yet, though I have wondered about being a full-time coach. I prefer not to sell webinars or programs, and though it's an idea I've not yet tried, I also see paid speaking as an avenue to develop and explore.

There's a need to clarify and hone my story and message. Ted's course helps with that, and it's in line with my training and learning. I wonder, though, who could or would want to use me as a mentor or coach? I'd also like to have a coach to help guide me, yet at this point, the closest person I have for a coach is my cousin Alex.

Pivotal street people have known I've not yet provided much up to August 2018. In the future, we thrive, yet I strive to choose and fuse to pay my dues. The clues developed along the shoreline rewind to *The Fountains of Yesterday* as a sign. Must I be money focused now? If my plow, our fields, and our efforts are to earn future yields, I must commit to the process to let our scenario unfold. I now know this journey includes vastly many more nodal points that just my wishes, my books, and me.

Diana had called and confirmed the gathering idea is a good one. She called it a '$5 idea.' Diana's guidance is helpful on this journey as she's patient, kind, and generous with her grace, information, and advice. I also love talking with her, and she's fun! The premise is that if each person in the Fraser Valley gave $5 a month, we could house all the people who need and want a home in that area. Two hundred fifty-three people are required to house and feed one person, a Yearly Seed, as a shared objective.

Open to Fate formed a lot slower than previous Fountains, and I'm concerned about how this glacial pace of text develops. I keep at it, yet I removed all my books from Amazon on February 12, 2018, for revision, and shifted the Share and Care cards' first earnings to be Patreon based instead of my books. The previous Fountains needed rewriting, though I still felt an urgency to provide; it's not a comfortable feeling.

It so often seems like I'm just at the start. We may be far from reaching the destination, though, in some ways, that's a positive thing. It makes me feel that although I've not achieved much, there is long-term potential. Perseverance is a factor, yet I also hope that it's me being perseverant and not delusional.

A program I value, enjoy, and recommend is Toastmasters. Toastmasters aid me with evolving my communication and are part of the journey to Full Seed. There are multiple pathways in Toastmasters, and the one I chose is Team Collaboration. I prepared a speech for the February 2018 area contest that is a series of words that explains my gathering and how it's to function.

I attempted to present my speech 'The Seed' and felt pretty awful about it. I tried to memorize the speech, though fell off course about 30 seconds into the presentation. I was agitated and solemn, yet I'm determined to make these projects prosper. I didn't recite the speech as intended though refused to quit and committed again to the process. To close this chapter, here is the address I wrote in full, even if I didn't successfully present it at the contest.

The Seed

Do you think that each person deserves food?

Do you think that each person deserves a home?

Do you think that each person deserves their necessary transportation?

If you think people do deserve that, how do you think we can help them have that?

Contest chair, fellow Toastmasters, and welcome guests:

I have an idea; it starts with a Seed

In a 2017 Report from by the Fraser Valley Regional District, 603 people were counted homeless in the Fraser Valley. Many people have complained about the homeless situation, though the homeless, I think, deserve our understanding, compassion, support, and respect. I write books, and in some of these books, I've written about an idea for a solution. The terms I use for this solution is the Seed Fund, and the goal is to achieve Full Seed.

Full Seed is the entire financial support for all those who need food, shelter, and transportation. A Yearly Seed, the amount required for completely covering these individuals is $15,128 per year. A Yearly Seed provides housing, utilities, groceries, and a bus pass. Welfare and PWD (A disability income) are existing supports, though some taxpayers complain about "people that don't want to work."

Some people cannot receive welfare or PWD benefits because they don't have a home address and some others who need help have been denied. Even for those that are on Welfare or PWD, the $375 shelter portion is not enough to afford a decent place to live. We should not force people to help. We can't push someone to be compassionate or care; we can, though, help germinate ideas and share them as seed bearers.

It starts with a Seed.

I've talked about helping the homeless and those in need for a while now. Through 2017, Providing Point, the program I started to share from the Seed Fund, provided $250 of gift cards to people on the street to different businesses; Safeway, Tim Hortons and the Yellow Deli. Though $250 is far from providing full coverage for the first Yearly Seed, it is a start. In one conversation with a friend named Tim, he suggested the idea of what would happen if every person pledged $5 a month towards providing for the Seed Fund.

This idea takes root.

If there are near 296,000 people in the Fraser Valley, from the 2016 Census, and each person put $5/month towards the cause, we could gather enough money to provide 1173 people with a Yearly Seed; almost twice the amount needed for the current homeless situation. As of now, through an online site called Patreon, Providing Point has two people pledging $5 a month to go to the Seed Fund for those in need. $10 may not be much, yet it is a start. I note we need additional supports other than money, though:

It starts with a seed.

The first three financial goals for Providing Point through Patreon are small; $50 a month, $200 a month, and then $867 a month. For $50 a month, we can provide five $10/month gift cards locally, for $200 a month we may provide 20x monthly gift cards, though reaching the third goal of $867/month, we move towards sustainability. A Share and Care card is a pair of linked cards where a Seed recipient may hold one, and then Providing Point holds the other. Providing Point puts money onto the linked cards to provide for Seed card recipients. As we earn more, the $10 a month evolves to

$10 per week and develop gradually forward to $50 per week for groceries. It is through these Share and Care cards that we can care for people's need for food.

What about shelter?

It's audacious to think that we can house every person who needs and wants a home, yet I do see it a worthy objective. If a Yearly Seed entirely covers a person's basic needs and is provided for by monthly contributions, 253 people can entirely shelter and care for a Seed recipient at $5 a month. Then again, some may pledge more.

I know numbers are a bit impersonal and may be overwhelming, though the math shows a possible solution. Some people pledge their time by volunteering, and that is helpful. Some can give their knowledge, skills, and expertise, and that is valuable too. For some, though, a monthly financial pledge is even more accessible and is a way to work towards helping those in need. The thing is, if we are compassionate people and want to help, we must step forward to do so.

It starts with a seed.

There are benefits to working together for a shared cause. We can make new connections and friends in addition to providing. We've learned and shall continue to learn much through Toastmasters as we learn how to convey our seeds to an audience. I know that most Toastmasters want to work towards a solution and though each of our clubs is a garden where we may live and thrive and grow, we should not forget what happens outside the walls of our club. We are called to be leaders and communicators and also to work for the betterment of our clubs AND our communities.

What would happen if the idea of the Seed Fund and Providing Point expanded outwards? What if other communities rallied together to support those in their areas and also achieved Full

Seed? Are the ideas of Providing Point and the Seed Fund something that would take root in the gardens of other cities and towns? Are there enough caring and compassionate people that will work together towards a shared solution? Ideally, the answer will be to provide for all those in need, though how shall we do it?

It starts with a Seed.

If our clubs are our gardens, I ask you to also to tend to the fields for combined yields for our communities. The journey of the Seed is a shared journey, and this speech is a seed from my garden. It's to remind us each that we can, do, and shall help others in our life and world. It also is a reminder that we are fortunate to be part of an organization, Toastmasters, that builds and develops pathways towards a shared and prosperous future. We each are seed bearers, and Providing Point is my seed. We cannot make a seed grow, though we can help it to become.

It starts with a Seed.

Here is where it sprouts!

A SEED TO A TREE

(February 27th, 2018 @ 6:44 PM)

This section, as most writing best be, is intentional. I wrote this section to share with people locally by printing it out to share in blue Duo-Tang binders. These few pages are meant to tell you what I'm doing and why, though it was much time before I completed the entire book.

The day before, the 4th Fountain rereleased on Amazon. I'd written seven of these Fountain books, though had taken them all off Amazon because they needed additional revision. I used this one, the 8th Fountain, as a process point to clarify and hone my work and intents. This section is used to condense my intentions up to now into a few pages to catch people up to where we are in the process.

I started writing the first book because of Natalie Imbruglia. When I was in the psych ward in 1999 and 2000-2001, the Natalie delusion and obsession was far stronger than it is now. In 2013, I started writing the first Fountain, *Finding Natalie*, with the intent to share the book with Earth and have her read a copy. The plan back then was for her to initiate a meeting with me, though this objective has drastically shifted since the first book.

The 2nd to 5th Fountains carried some ideas and notions about Natalie, and though I still think of her, meeting her is not the mission I hold strongest. It was in the 3rd to 6th Fountains where I wrote a bit about the Seed Fund and Providing Point and presented promises and my Income Declaration. The responsibilities shifted since the original releases of those books, and as of February 27th, 2018, the commitments were being restated and solidified.

We live here in the Fraser Valley, and we know many people don't have a home in which to live. We also know that many people that *do* have homes and jobs that are just keeping afloat. For me, I know that I'd like to have a car and a house, though, with my current earnings, I can't imagine how. I also sense some strong displeasure from others because I don't have a regular job and have the life I have and live.

Still, though, I want to make sure we as a community can provide for others on the street and in need and also others who need or want extra support. I've made a lot of promises and declarations, and though not yet fulfilled, I work to honour these commitments.

www.Patreon.com/Introversial is the primary gathering point. As of June 2018, we use all money gathered through that page for the Share and Care card program. We started with individual one-time $10 gift cards locally, though one of the next steps was regular monthly support. At the point of this book's release, we had $46/month pledged by seven different sources.

At the point of $650 pledged a month, we can provide fifteen people with $10 *a week* Share and Care gift cards from the Patreon earnings. The first goal of $50 a month is a small goal in the long-term objectives of providing for *all* people, though we know it starts somewhere. It begins with a seed.

I know I've been overtly money focused sometimes. It's because I know funds are a tool that we can use for others. A monthly $5 or $10 a month pledge is not massive either. $5 is 1% of a person's income if they earn $500 a month; it's even less than a quarter a day. If you went to a church and tithed, you'd need to give the church 10% a month, which is $50 for a $500 per month income. I remember, though, my goals are not a church.

Some people may contest they can't do anything to help the homeless. If 253 people pledged $5 a month to one person, that person could have $850 a month rent, $150 per month for utilities, $50 a week groceries, and a bus pass. Two hundred fifty-three people can care for one individual whose life would be drastically different. If every person in the Fraser Valley pledged $5 a month, we could provide 1,173 people with weekly groceries, a home, and a bus pass. Six hundred and three were homeless in 2017.

I have preached a bit about kindness and compassion, and they're values I hold. Some promote empathy, and that ability holds both understanding and compassion together. With insight, sometimes we can understand what it's like to be in a situation even if we've not experienced it, and since most people don't know what it's like to be without a home, it may be tricky. We still, though, can have empathy and work to provide people with a home. We need the kindness and compassion *in action* and heart in what we do for those people.

Many people in Chilliwack know I've been muddled up with this bookwork and promise to earn for others. I know I've not provided the first home yet and I've been performing a lot of the work on my own. I haven't earned much support with the purchase of my books, and I've not been actively seeking donations and pledges. I don't like mooching, and wonder if it's necessary.

I obsessively keep working because I know this does hold value. I know I can't force a seed to grow, and it'll be awesome and fantastic to get some help for us to germinate these ideas and let them thrive!

Other than money or books, how can people help? If you don't want to contribute money, you can offer your skills or time. In Chilliwack, Ruth and Naomi's takes in volunteers on the last Thursday of each month, and you can call them to sign up. The Salvation Army is also a place to help with the soup kitchen and volunteering, and a third place, the Cyrus Centre is, a program that helps with at-risk youth.

I bullishly believe that the best contribution I may make is to tend the seeds, plant some fields, and remember to help out others when I can. We need to gather together and work in our communities no matter where we live; things do not often happen magically. If we are compassionate people, we must step forward and do something. Sharing kindness or a 'hi' and 'hello' are also great things we can provide, and donating items that we have at home that we may not need can be helpful too.

As one person, maybe the best things I can do are be an advocate and share the seeds of giving and compassion. I've had a teetering balance between working for others, and also providing for myself, and though I've been working on books for about a few years, I've not found much income from books yet either. I keep at it though.

Regarding tending the public fields, we also must not forget to tend to our gardens. I remember Toastmasters is a place to gather seeds and share ideas and hearts and learn how to speak to a public audience. Both Wednesday nights and SnowPeaks on Thursdays are places to be and remind me our relationships are crucial and vital. We ensure we move forward and by sharing ideas and links, and some help could come from book sales.

My plotting and planning include schemes to have Chilliwack a place where we can and shall provide for people with my work. Though I've been with the books for a couple of years now, it's only in 2018 that I shifted into advocacy and also founding the ideas of NGOs to support. For those that are in lack or need, I want us to find people to help you.

Some friends think I'm a fool for wanting to help people, and some others think I best give my money to other charities. The thing is, I don't have money. When I can acquire some cash, I'd like to order copies of the books and share them locally. If it costs $80 to order a batch of 10-11x books, then selling them is forward motion, yet only at a small scale. I prefer to find a more efficient means of support.

If we as a community can work from within to outward for and with our audience, could we gather far more than just for our local community? Would other companies and creatives put their earnings, ideas, and practices into providing in their communities?

It's a fundamental premise; if each person put $5 per month to those in need, we can provide good lives for others who need and want a home. Some people may contribute more than $5 a month, and that'd be fantastic! I can't 'fix' this situation on my own; it requires support by pooling together.

Very few people have read my books up to release, and I accept that. I'll keep gathering, sharing, and tending the seeds to ensure we may make a better situation for all, and even if I don't have a clear elevator pitch to tell people why they should buy the books, I believe they hold value. They're not classified as self-help, business, or entirely about social causes, though like the pages you have here, they stem from my dissatisfaction with how life is and has been.

The books are also a conduit to share collectively how life can be, even if every experience *is* distinct and has its own parameters. The Fountains are written outwards to any who may want to subscribe to help other people or themselves, and though it's not a straightforward value proposition, the ideas hold merit.

The Fountains books started as a form and wish for Natalie, though they've evolved past that and how I use them for planning, processing, and also therapy. The Fountain's earnings are used partly for social causes and till some seeds for other people's lives and gardens. There is a hint for you; dream big and have a more substantial impact.

I'm happy, glad, and thankful that people read what I've written. It is an honour, a blessing, and an ultra-generous gift of time and attention. If I'm to gather from my books, though, I must use them for a benefit beyond my wants. Some people have other motivations and use different tactics to achieve their desires, though I intend to use myself thoroughly well to earn and generate a shared Freedom Solution; this is not only for myself!

If you want me to justify that position, I must argue that it'd be easy to earn a basic living just for myself. I could get a part-time job and ignore other people's needs, even my own. I see it as a massive challenge and more worthwhile to earn for many, and if I set my big hairy audacious goals to make enough to give away 99%, it gives me a much higher objective to expand. I know I don't need that much, yet I want to work and earn wealth.

It's also not fair for me to be wealthy if others cannot afford to eat. A lot of people would love to be rich; it's alluring and shared as an objective and element of freedom. If I have the opportunity and privilege to have my needs cared for, then I also must assure others too may reap similar benefits and rewards.

Setting massive objectives and far-reaching guideposts allow a long, arduous climb instead of just plateauing and accepting mediocrity. I work for others first. We must raise those who need a lift while also working with those that want to assist us in reaching our maximum potential.

Some may think it's me shooting myself in the foot before running a marathon to promise to help others, yet I want us to unify and work together. We need not put others down so we can reach the top, and we can lift some up when we level. I have a firm belief that by setting audacious and irrational goals, we can become that much more together than if we just set small targets.

At this point, some people might say, "It's not the destination; it's the journey." If I didn't set a faraway destination, then there wouldn't be much of a journey to get there. I know we're a long way away from housing the first person with the Patreon earnings, yet I still deem it a worthy and challenging objective to provide.

It's a lot different than when my first wish was to meet Natalie. Reaching that goal would be so much less valuable for others. Sure, I'd get to meet her and talk, yet if I set my primary goal as Full Seed (providing for all people) and *also* get to meet her, it shall be an entirely different conversation.

Natalie advocates for social causes too, hers is to end obstetric fistula, and I dare not forget that she's also working for many, and not just herself. If we work for others, we may hold a far more significant reward and effect than only earning only for our own basic needs.

Think now of the maple tree. The maple produces many seeds that slowly fall to the ground like helicopters. The trees take a long time to grow, though when they do become mature, they need not be destroyed to tap them for their sap. The vital life of the tree is not lost to make use of them for something that is explicitly enjoyable.

It takes many years to cultivate the forest, though the trees produce something of value like the slowly forming streams of text. Can this be attuned to the syrup dripping slowly like the waters of life that may also nourish? Why do their seeds take so long to reach the ground!? Well, maybe waffles would be sweet.

I cannot easily describe the Fountains books, yet the tones of them are disjointed. The way this section formed is similar to how I've been writing in the past two to three years. I commit to writing a chapter, often in one sitting, and let the waters flow out through the keys. Later I revise them, add some tidbits, and then revise again. The available Fountains have gone through multiple distillations before consumed.

I've yet to know how to describe my written work to others in a short sentence. The ideas are strewn and spread out across the fields of text, and by reading, you are helping with this work. You pick up the pollen from the open flowers and give a chance for seeds to form, germinate, and grow. The waters of life keep active to nourish the seeds; the Fountains are merely one source of water.

In time, the seeds thrive, and as we tend them and cultivate the production, we may save some seeds to plant in other fields and gardens. It starts with a seed, and these books are some seeds to share.

There's not always only one solution to an issue, and often a resolution may not seem possible. If we are to plant the fields for combined yields, I give Introversial's Patreon earnings and part of my book earnings to Chilliwack.

We must remember, though, that each community, not only our own, has people who need help. I want to create ideas and programs that can efficiently work in other cities, though where I started these books is in Chilliwack. I'm learning, developing, and evolving myself, my work, and my ideas and intents, and I tell you, Chilliwack has fertile soil. Let us grow!

WHAT DID YOU SAY?

Having an idea to choose is much different than following through with a choice. March 17th, 2018, I decided to leave Snowpeaks, though I may return.

I'm a waffle! I've had difficulty making decisions as they float in my mind for a few weeks before deciding. The concern I've had with some choices is how I go back and forth and restructure, like the 100% books to Seed choice I made and then reverting in February 2018. Later in *The Sands of Yesterday*, I recommitted 100% of the earnings from individual Fountains to giving and hold.

Such as it is, I chose to scoop from Snowpeaks; a Magic term for conceding. There's absolute freedom in making a choice, yet there also are the insecurities and doubts about consequences and the premise of it being a 'right' choice. Maybe it's best not to think of the decision as good or bad, or right or wrong, instead, merely that it's a decision made. I chose, I follow through, and I build as best as I can with that decision.

I've had concerns about choices because I'm afraid I won't be able to follow up with them. Over the previous two weeks, I'd had doubts about my books and creative process and was concerned about the lack of results of both the book sales and Patreon earnings.

I've been writing about Providing Point since the 4th or 5th Fountains without having yet breached the $50/month goal for pledges by May 2019. I know that noting my victories and wins is valuable, yet some metrics allude that I've been wasting my time.

Two key people I remind myself about are my cousin Alex and my friend Kyle. I'm aware they've cared for me exceptionally well, give me great support, luck, and grace, and have helped me by letting me natter and babble through my insecurities. Alex allows me to make vital connections and contacts enabling me a pathway of a more loved and hopefully enjoyed future.

We find ways to build and achieve, and with a conversation with Kyle, I committed to three things. One of the choices frightens me. The commitment I made is dual-layered and included something I've not done so well in the past; I decided to stop smoking inside to adopt a pet.

I've had trepidation about having a pet and not smoking inside because I've been a smoker for twenty plus years and fumed in my apartment. I don't want to smoke indoors and have a pet there because that wouldn't be fair to the animal. I still may smoke cigarettes; just they must be consumed on the patio. I'd like to have a home that is welcoming to non-smokers too, and by not burning inside, it allows me an apartment that doesn't wreak of smoke.

Before adopting Zeus, I found it difficult arriving home to an empty apartment and sometimes felt, as mentioned before, very insecure when I got in the door. It had been vacuous when I arrived, and with no pet, girlfriend, or roommate to come home to, it had been a challenge to get grounded and feel safe enough to think.

Two other kind and cool friends had just messaged. Visitors! They were on their way over and linked another critical lesson regarding money and friends. The advice and recommendation are not to leave outstanding balances of things or cash between people. If there is money owed, then repayment can be seen as the reason for contact and not the fact you genuinely like the friend. My Dad and Grandpa advised never to lend and never to borrow; it's a kind reminder of my past errors in judgment.

I feel happy and thankful for friends. I'm glad the two that visited received the foreign currency I got for them on my trip to Australia, though the outstanding debt with them put a wedge in the way of the friendship was. I feel happy, thankful, and relieved they attended my home regardless of the outstanding balance we had. I returned to this book after the visit with them.

We learned a new game during the friends' visit; Last Word Theorem. The premise of the game comes from the advice "Be the last one to speak." Being the last one to speak in a group is meant to guide and allow others to share what they have to say without interruption. It makes sure that each person has a chance to speak, though the game's challenge is to talk only when everyone else has spoken.

I explained the premise to my visitors, and it resulted in the three friends not saying a word for 15-25 minutes to not 'lose' by speaking first. A result of playing the game led to a parenting idea too. If the kids are too vocal, start the game and make sure you also don't say a word. It can lead to some peace and silence.

I found I'm awful at Last Word Theorem. I took the silence of the other three as a chance to play and be a continual 'loser' by speaking. I get tired of hearing myself talk sometimes, and that may be why I have few friends. Other people too may be tired of hearing me natter on and don't want to contact. A conscious thought, though, in groups to try not to talk until everyone else has spoken, and remember to speak up when it's your turn.

Gary reminded me again. I'm not doing the things I need to do to achieve my wishful goals. Even if happiness is a quotient of winning, I'm still not there. Or am I?

I've not put in the massive level of work required for Full Seed; that is clear, though with the idea to adjust actions or goals, how do I improve my behaviour? If to level up for my purposes, I don't want to submit and reduce my potential. Three primary things that Gary preaches and teaches are gratitude, empathy, and humility. I feel meek, thankful, and twisted up with sadness, wonder, and whist.

Winning is a kids game; boldly thriving is my objective. I subtly and underwhelmingly know that I'm breaking a lot of the rules and doing wrong and irresponsible things, yet the value I'm searching for with some is different. What are the benefits I'm seeking, for whom, and with what values?

I'm developing pathways of thought that are muddled, confused, decoded, and then awkwardly presented into books. I'm a sea urchin poking out my notions, fears, and insecurities into vacuous wastes of thought to find out if I can achieve an ethical Freedom Solution. I'm displaying the practice of shedding responsibilities and logic while also fusing my authentic thoughts and ideas into genuine appreciation and wonder.

My search is to explore as far into the future as I can while engaging in connection with experiences I have never lived before. Though in a social experiment that we seem to use, my objective is to create intrinsic value through a process of new thought, new ideas, and unique experiences.

I mix up the thoughts, I assume and consume new premises and theories, and then record it in my subconscious mind through language. I later fuse parts of the ideas with cryptic hints of and for more profound truth.

These books don't make sense to the world at this time. Maybe it's like my music. The linear timelines of spoken speech that then later attach precise meaning that I had zero intent or clues about ever knowing or predicting. Rewind to my job title; Contialitic Shoulsman. I explain this title as being highly cognitive and sometimes fused to a universal mind, yet I've also claimed part of my purpose is to provide. My faith and belief tell me that what I produce is who I am and what I deserve.

I present my thoughts and ideas through the written word, and I offer my creations and myself to those who I connect with and care. The chance and invested occurrences guide me too as we push towards the edge of time; the last lived moment of existence, which we call the present, lands us here providing future awareness.

Maybe I'm not meant to afford homes or money. Perhaps I'm just involved with doing what I do, have a bit of fun, and allow the future to unfold into natural order from what we've done and shall do. These preceding paragraphs shouldn't even make sense, yet they do. We can, in the present moment, choose to do or say anything we want to. We have that freedom because we can consciously decide to do anything; the permanency and long-term consequences are not always predictable though.

We each have the power of choice, and our fears of outcome may restrict us from doing things. Other ideas may be impulsive, and, considering the effects, could be a definition of crazy. Could us doing anything we want to without restriction or fear by pure impulse or automatic response allow us to be unlimited?

What is our natural behaviour? Are we following our authentic self in truth, or are we fusing confidence by doing anything we want to? I hope, with faith, we produce positive results.

If I try to force ideas or lessons on people and I don't know what is best for myself, let alone others, how will I attain the best results? Should I give up on my hopes, goals, and dreams (my future), or should I control how *I* live, think, and behave in the present and shift to full acceptance.

The 7th, 8th, and 9th Fountains are *The Fountains of Fortitude*. We slipped from the word Faith to Fate. Fate may just be accepting whatever happens in the future, though acceptance and choice in the present compared to the faith of imagining something that has not yet occurred.

We can think of language or specific words as temporal and directional links between the tenses of time. The notions of intent form a world where we aim to the future and land. What guides the accuracy of our landing?

Acceptance is a present based notion and includes the past from where we came. If we are warnings, can we also accept our fate and our destiny to think or believe we cannot change a thing? The only real moment of perception of new life is in the present, yet our past choices guide us in how we experience and behave within them.

If we can become entirely unaware or unconscious of the past, we also can lock ourselves into the present and become aware of bizarrely new things and thought. Because I was in this moment of being 'locked in the present,' I endured and formed these past 600-700 words of text not having a clue as to what I'm even saying.

The thing is, though, these choices, even if irrational, from a moment of the present that shall become the past. Since I publish, print, and share these books, the filibuster nonsense of this chapter may still hold some philosophical value. I don't know how these sentences will affect your mind.

Since I don't know how; that's how it's *Open to Fate*. A sequence of solidified moments held from existence into stone from the past. I wasn't there where you are, yet I'll also never be you in the same way you'll never be me. That moment has passed, and then onto the next.

So, yeah, if I shift my attitude and ethics to complete acceptance and also to fate and chance, subtle changes adjust the results. Tampering with the future is maybe a dangerous thing if it's a safety device. If the future is also in my control, I know I also best gain knowledge and not be foolish.

There's value in being honest and accurate, though honesty and sincerity sometimes link these books with what we think of time, effort, and energy. I don't know who's going to read them, yet weak faith calls me to want not to wish.

The value of being exceptionally accepting removes a desire to control, yet maybe it's also a pathway to peace and truth. We may act upon a stationary object, so if we value ourselves not to stay fixed and static, people may not control us. Forward motion.

Moving things is a way we may ward away acts of control, though my obsessive writing and forming of books isn't just a distraction. They are an attempt to remain as a lucid and unattached particle of being and result in developing and sharing ethics and intent.

The intent is often to convey profound ideas, yet I also must pause. When I think another is reading what I'm writing as I'm writing it, a projected belief communicates with the next moment of now. And yet then I don't want unintentional effects. How shall we unleash these unexpected results?

I cannot predict the future, and I remain accepting of consequences. Who we are, what we do, and the persistence of living long enough to see the future moments allow our results to find actual process and purpose. It's sometimes more enjoyable to interact with people instead of being solitary, though.

My feeling of guilt compounds in the past. As I've been acting freely and seeking happiness while shuffling off responsibility, I've also made promises I've yet to fulfill. I've rarely held stable employment, and authorship hasn't prospered up to now.

With Alpha Games, a local card shop, I'd been spending much time at the shop and hadn't worked on my books or gathered much seed. My guilty feelings stemmed from that. Some think happiness is the primary goal, yet maybe there's truth to that idea too? I love my life, yet note my joy is not perhaps a strong enough purpose for another even if it is a motivation.

I've been vacillating and shifting between ideas and draws of activity and attention, and for some months and a year or two, I obsessively focused on books and the Seed Fund. At other points, I've focused on relationships and communication, and I've been over-focused on earning money, even if unsuccessfully. I've also been prosperous while others have had lack.

I've held faith and hope in my solitary ramblings and ideas, yet my actions have at times been like a teenager. My consistent inconsistency has me concerned because I plant ideas and plans and then fumble into points of wonder. I'm baffled that I've been so oblivious.

I've shown a lack of concern and purpose, and partly, that's why I'm troubled. If I dissect my motivations and thoughts, can I regather and restore? If I've been active in enjoying life and people, I admit I also haven't focused on being engaged with work. I've seen some points of success, just not massive results in the metrics I had set as guidance.

I've been shifting and sliding, and it makes me wonder if I'm a snake in the grass. Should I be concerned society is a mongoose? Maybe it's a twisted analogy. What have I said? What have I done? The two questions don't line up.

I've said I'll gather for Providing Point, yet instead, I've been providing the points of assembling. I've been interacting with people and being an engaged friend rarely while sluffing off from working and earning for others. I've also, inversely been so focused on work and developing while not reaching out to connect. I've been too wound up and conscious for my liking.

Some people live their entire lives working just for themselves, and without a family, I may be being too selfish. When I do get to work on these books, then another layer hovers over my being; that I think my books are a waste of time.

The opposites of where I believed I would sell thousands of books and house people have shifted to me working on these projects as repentance for living a life I sometimes like or love. Saying I'm repenting for a living I love also calls a strange twist in the question "Why should I feel guilty?"

I answer that question. I've not lived up to my commitments to earning for Providing Point, I haven't been soliciting individuals, companies, and organizations for pledges, and if the books haven't sold, then I must discover a different pathway. If my shift from providing for others has gone back to building my life for me, I may need to recalculate.

I haven't yet succeeded in supplying homes, I've not reached selling books, and we have only forty-six dollars a month pledges to Patreon. That's a mediocre result of my efforts, though if nothing matters, why be concerned?

Well, I'm concerned, because I know it does matter. I'm going to need some help sorting this out, and I know I cannot do it all on my own.

THREE THINGS

If we are to succeed, we must be relevant. With me, it's the Seed Fund, the books, and my life. The Seed Fund is my purpose, yet my life calls for pleasure. I am quite hedonistic, yet compassionate guilt is also a core part of who I am. If I'm to provide, then I first must earn, though if I am to make money, then how? All the bundles and packets of advice I've seen or read blend into a neurotic self that still is wishing for clarity.

Simplification is helpful, and even if the previous chapter was obtuse and gnarled, it holds nuggets of truth. It's difficult to understand, though I've wanted to benefit people's lives significantly. A way to assist is to give advice, though some people don't want help or recommendations. Some people love being given information, while others don't and won't seek it out.

If my books hold good advice, which I'm not clear they do yet, people may want to learn from them and seek them out. If people are to seek out the books, then the books must be available, helpful, and in supply. All the layers cross-pollinate as we seed the fields.

My actions of working on my relationship gardens are meant to help the fields, and by exposing myself to social situations and being in connection with others, it helps share awareness of who I am too. My skeptical nature about self-promotion trips me up to call my books or music products, yet if I'm going to sell them, then I best call them by the units they are. If I want to earn from my creative work, then books and music are my products.

A twist with Providing Point and business terms shift differently, as I'm not providing for shareholders. My shareholders are those that are part of my network, yet more specifically, the individual community members with whom I wish to serve. That includes friends, yet friends should not be considered customers.

Providing Point's patrons are providers, and providers help provide for people; people that shall use the organization's services. My sporadic and inconsistent behaviours may be an asset to the process, yet by being fragmented and scattered through many different groups, points of time, and contacts, we gain a more extensive web of exposure.

I centred on helping Alpha Games with their card sorting for a few weeks, and some of the dregs (a term used by the owner of the shop) include a few who've processed some of my creative works. Selling my cards to Alpha Games also helped me order copies of books to share, which are a step forward.

The impulse to share the books is sometimes congruent with the recommendations of others to pursue my dreams and not give up. For the 4th Fountain copies ordered into town, they sell for $10 each with $5 to Providing Point and $5 to cover the cost of ordering them. From the copies of the March 21st batch, $97.20 went to Providing Point for sharing locally. This money was the first money that Providing Point shared in 2018.

Though my Dad doesn't like the idea of me ordering books, the urgency of providing is evident and selling books is a pathway towards doing so. It's not only my Dad that assures me I need to care for myself first before helping others, though, and seem to insist I'm doing this to care for me too.

I evade saying some things because of fear of judgment from my Dad, and I shall attempt to justify it. It may be a rationalization I wish not to make, though, because my Dad values self-responsibility and not so much sharing with strangers, I may be foolish to tell you these things. My careless actions for Providing Point show how I don't like pursuing the cause monetarily because I don't like asking for money.

I had an intake for volunteering at Ruth and Naomi's, a street-level mission for those in need, and that's a way to give too. I need more community involvement, and it seems I have my fingers in a few different pies. I quit SnowPeaks in March and have sometimes wondered about my writing. My reasons come from different motivations, though it's true the separate ideas, commitments, and activities can blend for multi-win purposes.

If the books don't sell, does that mean we can't reach Full Seed? Not necessarily. If the books sell, can we confirm the idea of Providing Point is a good one? Hopefully. If we sell books, can we share the thoughts and intents of the Seed Fund and garner more support? Yes. Is the program the right thing? I'm not certain.

The Fountains books are part of the Patreon rewards, and as people start to read the books, the incentive of purchasing copies can potentially increase patronship. The more patrons we have, the more we can give and share with Providing Point, therefore having a more significant impact. The more effect Providing Point has, the more critical the books can be, and by being inclusive and more consistent and connected, we can gather more people to work together.

Dad, you know that I've been persistent, and I know I've been foolish and obsessive. My books haven't yet sold, and I have bought copies to bring into Chilliwack. Having books to sell can earn me money too, and the February inversion of Patreon and Amazon sales commitments can assure a positive benefit for others. My firm belief is that by working for others *and* Providing Point can and shall guarantee an income source for me too.

My work in Chilliwack finds three things; we learn to live, earn to give, and mere wishes are filtered out by the sieve. As the Fountains have developed, I dabble in separate waters gathering the components, and though my scattered behaviours and thoughts allow the streams to form, we glean the streams of life, energy, and also income.

At Alpha Games, I tended some personal emotional and social needs, and I earned some survival money by selling Magic cards. I'd gotten to share my music, books, and codes with people, and I was allowed to help a liked and appreciated business owner with his shop. The benefit of gathering with various people helps shape the fabric of my creative work, and it's rad to be part of a life where our presence is valued and trusted. I don't always feel welcome, though, and wonder if I'm pushing my luck.

Ruth and Naomi's hadn't brought me on, though I still tend my needs to interact, understand, and meet people. As an extension of my work, goals, and objectives, it's best to know the people whom which Providing Point intends to help. Relationships are a fundamental human need, and functionally, I like to know how and what I can do for others.

And Toastmasters? I stayed with the Wednesday night group and chose the pathway of Team Collaboration. Toastmasters can help me learn how and where to share large-scale ideas to a real-life audience, and the response from the February 22nd speech reminds me that people do care about the homeless situation. An honest call for compassion may help if I can learn how to communicate the program; especially to those who can afford to provide monetary support. Learning how to speak to an audience will not only help clarify how to present the value proposition of contributing to help those in need, though also can expand the reach of our ideas.

I note another nuance here. In a meeting with Graham from Chilliwack Health and Housing, he noticed how I use the term 'we' when I was talking about Providing Point. Technically he's right, I was only one person working for the cause back then. I refer to what 'we' have done and are going to do like this work as a combined effort and not just myself. It is, though, we just haven't yet gathered all of the team and the components.

I've used the term *we* like this because it's a shared cause and not me alone. If people don't ally, maybe it is just my books and I. If people buy the Fountains, though, they are contributing, and as others join to provide through Patreon, they are part of the 'we' too. I am not attempting to be a saviour or messiah; it's a gathering of people together to help a humanitarian cause in our local community.

In recent months I've been very narrowly focused on my wants and not thinking so much of those in need. I've levelled up my thoughts and integration, though it's only here again I get outside the halls of my mind and outwards to other countries and worlds.

This is condensed into a unique nodal point, and still, thankfully, my intents start to breach out past the narrow confines of my mind. Thank You! Three in one is another allusion to how God works through us each as individuals. I thank Him for that reminder and send a wish and prayer we continue to guide my comprehension in this universe.

This chapter turned out to be a super short section, though, because the energy shifted. We cross into a new path.

ROBERT KOYICH

RESET THE FOUNDATIONS

I've felt like I'm wasting my life because I've not accomplished much. Even if some may say I wrote a few books up to now, I haven't found a girlfriend, I've barely had regular employment, and I've not secured a path of profitable authorship. A dear friend had called me back from earlier in the day, though, reminding me to be positive.

The disparaging pushes and pulls find me wanting to bitch and complain about my life when there is a lot of good. There are ideas to work with and earn a living, and I do have a home. There also are ever repeating patterns of feeling awful, not having much, and then diving into a pot of coffee to write books. I remind myself too that I also now have my cat, a bit of food, tobacco, and, sometimes, hope.

I want to earn my living yet show the gravity of not, however, finding a definite and pure purpose. My cigarettes are a distraction, the coffee seems to be my drug of choice, and then I remember I can write anything. I have obsessed about the Fountains and have an idea they may matter.

If I can write valuable ideas and premises that can change the fabric of decency into ordinary cloth, what does it matter if no one wears it? People know I've been weaving tapestries, yet the walls of my soul here are sometimes bare. My impulsive urges occasionally have called me to self-destruct and shred paintings like a lucid artist.

I climbed high and hopeful thinking of my dream girl; then reality pushed me back down the slide to the bottom of never. Not forever as I thought it was, yet still the ever-constant awareness that I'm here and haven't accomplished much. I was two cups of coffee into these pages, knowing I committed to six hours of wakefulness at 9:42 PM. When I did so, I got excited about writing and said: "committed to the process" like a declaration of worth, and then, shouted like a person about to be locked up in the psych ward.

During the three weeks before I had been smoking inside. A choice to smoke on the patio instead came from the idea to adopt Zeus, and as the cat is to live in my home, I must not smoke inside. I also acquired another buffer for my being in 2018; I now have a TV and Netflix at home.

I watched a documentary about the spacecraft Voyager, and it cued vague ideas of what was happening when my parents conceived me. The notion that people use rockets as a metaphor for ejaculation made me wonder if my parents imagined me at the point of Voyager 1 or Voyager 2 in 1977. I was born in May 1978.

The Voyager spacecraft left Earth to view the other planets in our solar system, and when I saw the first recorded images of Jupiter, they seemed like a hallucination and painted deceit. The flat Earth people have nothing on the premise that all is a mere figment of our imagination. Some people believe everything outside of them is a hallucination. It's an idea called Solipsism.

My imagination also has fooled me to believe that everything outside of my consciousness is a delusion. I've even thought that everything I perceive is a direct and immediate sign relevant to me. I've held these beliefs semi-frequently when writing, yet my desire for financial results requires there to be others to process what I have formed. My awareness of having achieved little through my work, though, shows support for the delusion.

In moments of solitary awareness, inceptive messages, emails, and 'bling's from the phone surgically incept my consciousness with deft synchronicity, and these sounds from my phone seem to inject ideas and awareness into my mind surgically. Spinning to psychic impressions, I can sometimes anticipate these sounds before they occur; however, I cannot predict the future.

The people that can plan months or years into the future successfully hold a high power that I lack at this point. The persistence of keeping pressing the keys and slugging the cursor across the page with woven ideas is a skill, yet how will it be appreciated if there's no one to perceive it?

My wants are few, yet I've been setting goals to give myself something to work towards with life. With sorting cards at Alpha, I could earn some cash, yet purchasing cards was a lure too. I wanted to invest and buy and sell Magic cards again, yet it's a dangerous lure to chase a return. A strong urge of profit can draw action, though, and those that want to earn money can find ways to do so. The thirst, though, for money concerns me.

With my books, they also seem to tip me forward to spill a drink. I've wanted to order printed copies to sell books, yet when I get money focused and profit-driven, I seem to stifle myself. Some people may want money, go out and earn it, and then revel in having massive or comfortable amounts of income. That's one way to prosperity. I'd also like to make ethical earnings and not through coerced sales or forced labour.

Someone buying a copy of my book is, in some cases, a gift of them sharing love or appreciation. Oppositely, I like to share with others to show my love, likeness, or recognition. It's true that some sales and pledges may come from sharing the books, so I wonder if relaying copies of my work may draw awareness, authentic care, and legitimate interest.

Those who read the books may glean compassion and share with the causes mentioned in the books, and others may find interest in understanding. Through reader recommendations, *The Fountains of Fortitude* have shown that my wishes were the sand I was building on. I fell back into realizing that only a rare few care about my hopes, goals, and dreams.

Just like me, some people want sure things and not whimsical fancy. I may have gone into the oceans from the salty shoreline, yet it's more explicit that I've found I don't want to only sit on the beach. I desire a life amongst the other wildlife and not to sit at home and burn. Trepidation dissipates, I pray we find prosperity, yet still, I hold an edge.

Coffee is substantially an issue for me. The late nights I've spent working in the fields of text are my responsibility as well as tending the soil on public grounds. My work is like a commune, and that word links to an idea from January 2018 when I was visiting my Dad. He commented that he thinks I'm more of a socialist than he is. That statement is true, yet let me extrapolate.

I believe in a universal basic living income. Income need not be a wage, yet the majority of the population believes that people should have a job. An Italian saying is *chi non lavora, non mangia*. The translation is 'Who does not work does not eat,' though if that is true, I hope to work enough to earn for others to eat.

My Dad thinks me socialistic, yet I know I'm positively money focused sometimes. I thought of two terms; calling someone a social capitalist or a capitalizing socialist. I can be the social capitalist working and earning money for others and myself and then provide so we all can have good things. I also don't want to a capitalizing socialist grabbing at free things without earning them.

Gary's premise of meritocracy is right; I must work to earn my money and not mooch. I also have empathy for those without and wish my books to be a conduit for providing and receiving. I know I don't have massive amounts of income for myself, yet an abundance of resources would be grand.

If I earn excess, I don't see it as an obligation to share; it's reciprocation. Giving in the future is partly because of my gratitude for being allowed the life I live now. I'm don't feel entitled to have what I have, yet am profoundly thankful to have such. I use my ability to give because of gladness, and yes, a bit of guilt, yet appreciation of having things is a motivation to give to others; especially those for whom we have compassion or care.

Since I've made bold claims and goals that I haven't yet reached, I press on and endure. A conversation with a friend almost had me entirely give up on the books and Providing Point on March 29th, 2018. The friend gave me lots of input and advice, and a lot of what he said holds merit and value. From the conversation with him, I mutated help and guidance while blending wisdom.

I shall not give up on the books or Providing Point; I do, though, need to form some repentance from my bold wishes and proclamations. I keep creating the books and releasing them, though the most important take away from the conversation with the friend might be to release the attachment to rely on the financial gain from authorship. I don't need to stop writing or working; I need to release my obsession of needing to earn from my bookwork.

If I can create for value and interest, release my projected expectation or need of a monetary return from my authorship, regather, and then honestly care and tend people with love, perhaps we do find an alternate form of a mutually positive future.

I started writing another project during the formation of the base of this chapter. The text is called *Nodal Input* and launched from a conversation with a dear friend. The premise of the document is to share my Magic codes and invented language openly. *Nodal Input* includes the Mox code, Planeswalker referencing, and my understanding of social parameters based on mathematics and perception. Colour referencing and group dynamics are part of the systems, and there's also some personality theory and explanation.

The audience base for *Nodal Input* is exceptionally narrow, yet I'd like to share the concepts. The friends I labelled Planeswalkers help me hone in on truth and are beneficial for my understanding and trust, and I'm thankful our subvert understanding clarifies. Secrets and codes reveal the multiple attempts of deception and abuse.

With mental stimulation, a conversation can be an involved and substantial thing, and if we combine ideas of block-chain technology, think of each friend as a database of all they know about us. There are different data points and input; what they hear, what they've seen, what memories or impressions of us they have. Though we're always the same person, there's so much known about us from other viewpoints, even if each of us the same person from start to finish.

Some friends know how we feel, smell, and in rare cases, even how we taste. If each person is a separate database of our input, then think of the networking capabilities and cross-referencing when we bond. With books, codes, music, and our points of view, there are multiple base points of each of us in the world.

My recordings are theoretically the same base set of input as the books cement as solidified works. The threads of codes, contact, and connection weave in the music and books, yet the individual people who've heard or read them are processing centres of their own.

The way I feel and perceive others may not convey accurately. Many could presume what they think from their own belief, yet mental deception is a real thing. We don't all know the abuse or challenges others have gone through that make them who they are, and there is a core of who we are *and* how we exist. That theoretically is unique and not necessarily understood entirely by anyone else. What about the premise of God, though?

The idea of universal omniscience is a different way to think of God. Linked to a previous Fountain's ideas of G.O.D. as being the Global Organized Directive or the Galactic Organizing Directive, compound the concept of God as knowing absolutely everything; a Galactic Omniscient Deity.

Consider that every letter of this book, and other publications, has been explicitly compiled without consent from the authors. I may think I've written my books, yet the surgical implants of inceptive editing, the points in time when we read, and the consequences of what happens if and when the information processes are beyond my control.

The two words, *fate* and *destiny,* also hold different connotations. We can consider fate as an outcome that was meant to happen. Destiny can be a wish for future events to pass and then become a reality, and once happened, can be considered fate. It was fate that we met on a plane of existence that holds more than just Earth. It was destiny that allowed the moment of the present to unfold to let the bold choice enable us to wade amongst the moment of now.

Each grain of sand holds a crystalline structure moulding form and position as a static point and place of time and space. Every moment we experience is now, and all that happened is the fate foretold that we could recall in the present.

Anything you remember in the future is destiny unfolded, even if you may or may not have wished for it. Every event of the past must have occurred to allow the moments you become aware of to be in this exact moment. I form the warm drink to link the swarm of ink into the pink lighter's ignition, yet wishing upon a star that she precisely knows who you are.

We all can make choices, though; free will is a thing. The trip is that no matter what we do, we move into new moments that cannot be any different than they are according to the parameters of what happened before. How do we now allow ourselves to choose to fuse the moments of rhyme?

Our paths may be narrowly affecting and redirecting all the other timelines from their placement next to our actions and ourselves. We can divert a linear or direct approach, yet twine back to the premise of linear time theory is that all things are unidirectional. We can't reverse real life, yet we can modify the consequences. It's a trip, and one I wish not to leave.

SIGNS FROM THE UNIVERSE

Am I devoted to the cause or a stubborn mule? Hold the fabric of time with the dramatic climb down with truth and love, and with the rhymes above the dove's passion starts to flow to below. Set the net to abet the Jet and remind the merchant that Gary's nowhere near done yet.

The sun began to rise again when the lies found the pad and pen pressing the keys to the lion's den. A hen calls the cow back to the plow, and to quote Toby Keith, "How do you like me now?"

People can, now, legally smoke green mana (marijuana) in Canada, and I'm still not able to do so. I'd love to smoke pot again, though I also know the consequences; hospital, insanity, and restrictive poverty. Understanding the implications of how marijuana is for me keep me from doing so, though there's also paranoia and a near inability to talk; that's bundled in with the insanity.

Blue mana can be tears, meth, and water. Blue mana represents intellect and deceit also and isn't always kind, yet sometimes necessary for survival. I know I'm not a general and don't want to command troops, yet it seems that the war is going on. Even with subvert ideas that I shouldn't know, I'm thankful for the Apple links.

I'm grateful for Dad and Sarah too and glad I have books to form and read. There may be a substantial benefit by returning to reading to learn and expand, and it's also an investment to make more time for language learning.

Red mana links to primary, visual, and battling people. I shall not lose my fire as we cultivate my passions and desires to thrive. While the Ruby Loverock and Primary Lovestone hold the node, it's best we fuse allegiances and honour the Sprites too, even if they're green.

White mana links to forces, instincts, and systems. A Bant (green, white, blue) focal point conducts a single node in the Contialis. With an adept reach like an urchin, some carry the sequences and series digitally. As we evolve, adaptation becomes valuable, and my books and work come to make sense. In many things, such as the ideas of religious unity, the worlds of nature and technology merge, and the shoulic blend of all people and language are also noded.

Black mana twists the ciggies, sound, and life while Mooshka may deepen mental stability. As part of future Fountains, the relative lines of an Emerald add to the former crewmates and also foundational seed people. I was getting closer to tossing away the smoking habit and addiction, though it fell back in strong upon returning from Australia.

My home smelled pretty atrocious from smoking inside, yet I don't forget the outer space links from Mox Jet associations. It's clear the airwaves hold some clouds and a few people told me I should shift genres or the medium I've been using. Andrew recommended visual art, and Opal Sprite suggested taking up pottery. Why would I change to entirely unknown art forms if the objective were to hone existing skills and form a creative profession? Is it resisting a different path, or mastering this way of writing?

Considering how many people have read my books, I'm not clear that there's a large enough sample base to deem the books worthy or not. Opal had asked me about my marketing plan, and bizarrely, I could articulate my current project. Still, I carried the agitation from the results shown up to that point. Opal told me, "You're twitching," and that may be a sign I'm still over-obsessed.

Deep layers of poor choices seem to fuse into the meld. Thankfully, I'm living on Earth, even if another human thought I'm of otherworldly birth. Maybe I should shift to baffling linguistics and compound the parameters that explain the confusion. If I can form or decipher a long string of information, is it dangerous to convert it into plain English?

What would happen if I tried to infuse and mix with false

ideas, premises, and theories? I honestly would prefer to help enlighten people to the truth, though what if I've been misinformed and misguided; even if unintentionally? Does this mean I should put the keys away and learn to pray, even if in a non-religious and secular way?

If the crucial pieces of information are mentally leaked when I write and form these books, does that explain how they have a function cognitively and telepathically? Even if no one else reads them, I'm attempting to gather and guide. I want to provide, and I also don't want to mooch or borrow time, money, or grace. If I'm meant to be alone and isolated, I'm still delighted, fortunate, and grateful to interact with the rare few humans that talk to me.

I've gone through possession before, and I've written previously about how I used to transform into other people and feel like I was entirely them. I'm also now wondering of outer space and if my delusional beliefs are fusing elements of the cosmos that are meant to be secret.

I know how I'm only one entity and explicitly not in a dream world, yet the beliefs of others would skew and twist my mind into believing their truths instead of the core of who I am. Do you note how you can't openly express to another your core truths sometimes?

How are these the *Fountains of Fortitude*? They have drawn delusion, fantasy, and utterly illogical thought and sequences of words from my keyboard. How can there be fortitude with such obscure ideas as the foundation to hold them? Building a house upon sand is awful. What if I've been creating my universe upon illusions that would make sand seem surer than a titanium base?

I saw the movie *The Infinity Wars* the day I wrote this. It was strange. There were moments in the movie theatre that I'd seen from dreams much time before seeing the film in real life. Another friend a few days prior told me about how they don't know when they're in waking life or in dreams. When they don't know if they're awake or dreaming, they can perform actions to decipher if awake and in reality.

I almost always understand when I'm awake or dreaming. More lucidly, I remember when I'm awake and have imagined something before. Imagination can take us to exceptionally fanciful points of life, and some online mentors and life coaches recommend visualization to activate our minds; to create the experiences we want.

If fear is the guiding energy or thought, though, I warn you not to accept your believed fate. Hope, faith, and belief are positive when coupled together, yet I intuit that fear, confidence, and uncertainty can be potently dangerous too. When a person's energy shifts to a negative place, it's even more crucial to slow down, breath, and reassess.

What am I trying to achieve? I had focused on Natalie, success, and the Seed Fund, yet the results up to when I wrote this seemed to call for me to instead go down a path of destruction. I put alcohol in my tea when I wrote this, and I must not corrupt the energy of this work. Weirdly, my cigarettes call me back to a neutral balance as I paused to get a cup of water instead. I shifted from sadness as the first emotion and attempted to settle into a reset point.

The process of forming this text reminds me we need other people as a ground wire for ourselves sometimes. We need an outlet for our negative or potential negative energy to dissipate it from our souls. Not our spirits; those, I hope and pray, are unchangeable and hold the vital data of who we indeed are.

Our minds are not ours alone to know. The potential of other people's thoughts or actions to change the ideas that reside in our consciousness hold power; yet shall we produce good or bad. A pure spirit can change the fabric of the mind with inceptive contact, so please heed your intuition.

You know yourself better than I, or anyone else, and can tell who you are and how you feel. People may attempt to change your actions and beliefs, yet cross-reference them with your truths and awareness. Don't believe everything everyone tells you. Don't presume real everything you think.

Some may be lying or acting on false information and are unaware of your real truths. Preserving our core is vital, and voicing our truths may be necessary to regain and hold our integrity. When you grasp hold of yourself and become stable, it's the time to assert what's in line and accord with you universal purpose, function, and truth.

Do you hear voices? I don't mean the sounds of others that are real audible spoken words in the space you are within; I mean the inner nudges and inklings of truth or even the bossy commanding voices that tell you what to do.

Some people know of their conscience and the guiding recommendations that say, "don't do that" or "do it." Some other people have ultra-negative commands that could lead to or from insanity. Oppositely some may have voices they hear in their mind that are of loved ones that passed away.

When I was in college, I wrote a paper about if we can know another's mind. My argument was that we could never comprehend all of *our* thoughts, so how can we ever know entirely what *another's* account is. What I want to dredge is my self-awareness so that I can have an entire understanding of my being. I'd like to know and comprehend myself so well that I can know explicitly what is me, what is not, and then tell another.

I was diagnosed as a paranoid delusional schizophrenic, though my most recent diagnosis is undifferentiated schizophrenia. I have difficulty, sometimes, knowing what is other and what is me. Some people believe that every thought we hear in our mind is only our own, though I don't hold that belief. I believe in telepathy and crossed views, and if the premises of God by any religion infuse, then we know it's not all ourselves that created the world.

Some people posit that each of us is God, yet I don't agree with that. I know I'm not omniscient and ascribe that quality to the Global or Galactic Organized Directive. In a universal consciousness theory, God knows *all* things. How does that apply to something entirely unknown?

Theoretically, there may be some things that are entirely isolated and not in the conscious knowledge of any living or non-living being. Omniscience would know of the unknown too of all people and creatures. With humans, we don't do some things in *any* of our conscious minds as there are still things not yet discovered or created. The premise of omniscience is that those things *are* known; *all* items are known via omniscience. *All* includes the consciousness of other animals and plant life too and the entire past, present, and future.

I'm nowhere near omniscient; of the knowledge pool of Earth, I barely know anything. I'm just one single node in the Contialis, and though I may have a vast amount of self-derived notions and thoughts unique and personal to myself, outside of myself, I know so very little.

I don't even know many mainstream pop-culture references that are substantially common knowledge to many people. I may be an obscure reference point that few know of, yet as people come to know my work, my ideas, and me, a diffusion of me seeps out into the world. I must assure, by my responsibility to Earth, the cosmos, and time, that what I create is beneficial.

Or is it best I remain obscure and unknown? Is what I write vital? For many, it's not. That may be why few people have read or understood me. We can't force the rest of the world to follow ethical principles, and I don't know what the best thing or right thing is to do for the globe. I don't often even comprehend what's best for myself.

It is a responsibility to tend to the world, yet I need to heed wisdom and acceptance. From a thought in my mind when forming books a few months ago, I was told by an inner voice that I have no control over even the sequence of words I use, let alone their results.

Free will is a luxury some have, yet I desperately wish to channel into correct patterns and activities. I don't have free reign to do what I want to do, and I have lacked faith. I'll make the right choices. My hedonistic pleasures and desires could take me to destruction, though, and I don't want to rely so heavily on grace and forgiveness.

The miraculous happenstances of chance and fate have

served me well up to now, so to the Higher Powers, I pay homage. Mia amica contialitica, siamo entrambe pazzi. You know you, and I forever will think I have.

12:36 AM, May 2nd, 2018

Forty years on this planet. We are grains on the shoreline of rhyme. In time, we climb into the view of how I wish you knew that I thought I had a clue. It may be the technology that made me obsess of you, Nat, yet a lie it may be to say I ever see.

As a close to this chapter, without claiming any religious terms or deities as truth or fact, I send out a secular prayer as a wish to skip across the pond. Though it's not yet dawned on the day, let me learn to thrive so well I can create the ways to say I can never stay a day away. When the voice chooses to make my heart pray, it started with play. I look into the world to find some things discretely and inwardly curled, and I'm thankful that the years have unfurled.

Thank You, God, for letting me live. Thank you, Mom and Dad, for giving me birth and life, and thank you to the friends, family, and community that allow me to live this. I ask all of you that my life isn't even halfway complete.

Merci to the forces that be for eternity holds the key. I can never claim to be the strength of the world under the control of what I wish to see. Let our lives be free to assure we let the ocean meet the Sea. Amen.

A NEED TO CHOOSE

During the three weeks between when I wrote the previous chapter and this one, I'd not felt so well. I've been riddled with insecurities, apathy, and doubt, yet still, am thankful to be alive. I spoke with Chandra earlier in the day and told her how I feel I lack purpose and motivation in my life.

My sleep had been erratic with wake up times in the afternoon most days, and I didn't feel inspired. My belief in the bookwork had been near nil, and I wonder again if I'm not persevering, yet instead, I am delusional. The nagging feeling somewhere in my body, though, fuels the obsession to create even though it's not rational.

Regarding the premise of value not always being a monetary thing, I still felt poor sometimes. I don't think I've built books or work that shall form a legacy, and it's instead felt like I'm selfishly and bullishly shaping books with no substantial purpose.

This section may seem to be like a pity party, and I don't mean to be a Debbie Downer. I also write, sometimes, to run the feelings through my being as an attempt to cleanse and refresh my mind and attitude. I've thought my life and words are being corralled and channelled into pathways, not all my own, and religious tones of thought seep into my concerns attempting to give me hope and faith.

If all things are destined to occur, then does that mean I have zero choices in the matter? I may need to be patient to allow the course of events, though the precise results of my efforts are what drive me into feelings of hopelessness. My wishful mind tries to counteract those feelings by giving me the notion that I have a purpose.

When I think or judge what I'm creating isn't going to be processed, that's sometimes what's made me feel I've wasted my efforts. For my work, and most of my life, I've thought I'm smart, yet I also could accurately be called stupid or a fool.

When I try to force or push to have a knowledge-based purpose, there's a want to tell you recommendations about how to improve your life. If my life is not in order and thriving, though, how could the advice I give help you? It may because your life is not my life, and your outlook and mindset may be in a more positive state.

Maybe you're open to gleaning insight and activating the lessons I've not been able to use correctly in my life. Perhaps I should go back to some foundational blocks and intents; to make a restatement of what my wants and objectives are. These statements also must be honest and real, and not what I think I *should* do, though what I genuinely desire.

I want to continue living, I want to engage in more human interaction, and I want to remove some of my self-defeating behaviours. I also honestly don't want to quit smoking or stop writing and shaping these books. I want to have fantastic results from my writing while not needing to focus or think about marketing or sales, and that statement, to me, could be said as "I want the results, yet not have to put in the effort."

Up to now, the natural course of events has had me write a lot, and I should note that too. I *have* written a few books, and they *are* an accomplishment. My attachment to financial results, or rather the lack of them, is what's troubled me. I've also been hooked up on wanting to share the books, though don't know how they benefit another. They have been very self-focused, and I don't think the Fountains are relaying a solid value proposition to potential readers.

This section reminds me that I've been too focused on what I want. I need to focus more on what other people want, or rather yet, what I can do for other people that will benefit them.

Secondary gains are an idea I've had. The notion of secondary gains is supplying or providing for others and then receiving the secondary benefits from my right and just actions. It's a form of a trickle-down idea that means if I give up on pushing for purpose and act rightly, that positive benefits shall be the results. If my Mom used to tell me "behaviours have consequences," it may be time to adjust my behaviours again.

What do I do that helps or improves the lives of others? The first answer I have to that question is, "be their friend." If I'm over-focused on my work and isolated at home in the middle of the night working on books, that may not be a win for anyone. If only a few read the books I write, could that still be a benefit?

I need to be cautious of interacting with people that have the intent to hurt me too. My neurotic twist wonders if I've been reacting because I've had negative thoughts and have been thinking about how others can benefit me. I have been, at times, selfish and greedy and have had a lack of compassion and decency. I need to adjust how I've been behaving and what I've allowed in my mind.

My financial lack has been a factor, yet that's also my responsibility. I haven't always been working a job, my books haven't sold, and I've not made many positive reciprocal relationships that remember the premise of win/win. I've been thinking about my gains without thinking about what I can do to improve our situations with a bit of love and care.

There was a focal point in my heart the morning I wrote this. I felt some of the most profound sadness I've felt in the past three to four years when working on the book *Etched in Stone*. Since I've never met Natalie and had a conversation, the ideas and delusions fortify in my awareness as something I can't prove or entirely denounce. I remind us all that I cannot ever claim who it is I've felt in my soul and spirit. It may not be a famous singer.

It's like I'm a boat travelling down the river that is attached to a pier, and what I really should understand is the depths of how much I can care, and not attribute the feelings to a specific person. I honestly don't know who Natalie is, and it's compounded further by the question: "How could she ever know who I am if she's never spoken to me either?"

So wishes and fortitude remove the fantasy and reset the

lure that they use. A fusion reaction of stellar natural attraction nearly put me in traction for thinking of love. I cannot claim who is the dove I'll dwell with, yet the Ith holds the myth of what she believes in the weaves of text.

What times have her and I even had? Is there even one moment of life that she has experienced me? The tree of self revives the shade that lets the Spirit wade in the drink of what we think. I wonder if I should write from my future five-year me again like how I wrote in *Seeds of Tomorrow;* a chapter from my five-year future self. It's a reversal process to write back to the moment of then.

Maybe I need to write to the energy and spirit that I sense as Natalie and make sure that Nat is a lie. Perhaps Coleman is right, and the real love that cares for me as much as I had Nat is out there on Earth wishing me to know her real name. Have I mislabeled the spirit in my heart?

What happened to Demma? We were real love, I think. I liked her a lot and wonder if she's sad or angry I didn't keep in contact. She was a remarkable, vibrant, and beautiful, yet I've not thought of her often or as strongly as Natalie. I remember how I loved life when Demma and I were together. We were happy and had fun while Natalie has sometimes been sadness and despair. The keys speak to me through the words I see. She said "no," yet I don't know which one mentioned it.

I've felt riddled with doubt in my isolation. I could call out and ask the ones I love about who my lovestone is, yet I'm sure they don't know either. I don't understand how it is to live together, and as I clear the webs of deceit and how they want me beat; the laced treat holds the breath that keeps seeping tea into how I don't know who's for me.

In the keys, the next day, my awareness shifted to how I need to plan for the future, and not just a relationship. I need to know how I'll earn money to afford to live the life I desire. With the results yet shown from working on books, I'm not sure authorship shall be profitable; it certainly hadn't seemed that way up to early 2019.

My concerns also reminded me that buying and selling

Magic cards potentially was a money and greed path for me. Writing books may not yet have been an income source, yet their social value is higher than only focusing on money. I lost out on my Magic friends by quitting the game. Can my books help other's lives too? Do they hold a purpose more than just a monetary quotient?

We see reading through this that my love life is a concern, that my financial lack is bright, and socially that I've also had issues. It's seemed that I'm a focus of conspiracies and negative attention, and because of how insecure I feel out and about, I'm inclined to stay home at the plow; resting well while passively working on the books. A strong intuition tells me to do that since I'm not working full-time.

Some seem to be upset at me, like when I was at the welfare office. I seemed to sense there are plots and plans of which I'm the focus, and my fears of explanatory power and attention mustn't overwhelm. Maybe it's an excellent choice to be a homebound soul instead of pushing myself out into the community. Each of us must make decisions about how we shall live, and when I fear the criminal activities and energy towards myself, I seem to neglect how love and life may be gathered and built.

I know I can't please everyone, yet my desire to be alive and do something worthwhile calls me out into the world. I thought to make a book of thanks to people I knew before Chilliwack because I want to acknowledge my appreciation to my positive past. I might neglect to mention some names or people, though there are needs to choose.

Each of our lives is the consequence of a series of choices of both our own and others. Our attitudes source from how we've responded to those choices, and it's nice to think we can guide how we live our lives. Our consequences of an action are valid, and our decisions affect our current day realities.

I don't have a car because I don't work full-time to afford one. I don't have a girlfriend or a regular friend group in my home because I've not sought out or tended relationships very well. I've been a smoker for 24-25 years, and I remind myself that it's a choice too. I've often chosen pleasure and self-gratification over long-term planning and the requirements to lead a long, healthy life.

My decision to avoid some things and people may not resolve issues, so I process words to help allow stability. I can tend to and work towards correcting my behaviours, and my choice to not smoke marijuana or other drugs keeps me closer to sanity and out of the psych ward. My decision to join and stay with Toastmasters allows communication skills and confidence that improves my ability to speak to people.

My opportunity to write allows clarity and a potential pathway to shared prosperity and success, and even if I choose to curtail some things, there is the opposite pull of wanting to dive deep into coffee and all-night writing sessions. Instinctively I adapt and make the right decisions.

Another weird set of choices I make is which words to type or how I edit and distribute the books. When anyone reads one of my printed books, you see a linear sequence of text I've adapted and modified. There are multiple versions of the Fountains, and though the ideas are similar, subtle and significant grammatical and contextual corrections develop.

A book is a harmonious exposition of a series of choices, and my determination to form them solitarily also is a decision I've yet to comprehend. I think I have limitations and restrictions while the Law of Attraction and Success Coaches advocate we can do anything we want. They tell us we can achieve any goals we set, though I need to know what I want. It's encouraging to believe and also be rational.

Where we are and what we hold as a start point is different for each. As you see with me, I have decades of poor choices and actions that I need to rectify, so I shall. It's a conscious effort and commitment to be determined to adjust some of the things I do.

I'm open to receiving miracles, blessings, and peace, and we can choose love over anything. If we do, I hope we add respect and unity too. Think of where you are now, yet don't always think of where you need and want to go. Think also of what is pleasant for you in your current situation and gather more of that.

I love being at home with friends and also working on productive things. If I allow myself to do so, I can keep my heart, mind, and soul in the plow and stay open to connections with people. I cannot put my love in other people's gardens without permission, though. I can, though, cultivate a pleasant and beautiful garden and find others that want to develop, grow, and build with me.

Maybe it's best I don't go out trying to plow the fields. If others can do that far better than I can, then perhaps my value is to give them some useful seeds.

FRACTIONALIZED REALITY

(This section is from a thought experiment cued by Christy
Whitman as a response to a question about Heaven on Earth;
before and after I watched her video)

Before the video:

I'm not definite that I understand Heaven. I cognitively get
that people can live in liberal heavenly states while alive as
humans on Earth, yet I also think globally. Religious
contexts guide me to recall those that have passed on, and I
remember Christy's QSCA (Quantum Success Coaching
Academy) show; she had an episode with a medium named
James Van Praagh. James communicates with those passed
on.

I don't understand the afterlife and don't think of the dead
often in my conscious mind. I do, though, have belief in spirits
and invisible energies, entities, and actions. I believe there are
spiritual realms that crossover here on Earth, yet the cliché
view Heaven being of a Utopian society too is a notion. The
world of dreams also has had me in a few
reincarnation scenarios I've dreamt, and I'm not clear yet
about nirvana and non-living realms.

I'm an incredibly immediate reality person. What I mean
by that is that I'm almost always neurotically conscious of
being in the present. I rarely think of the past and am not so
often envisioning the future. If I slow down and process the
question: "do you think creating Heaven on Earth is possible?"
I'm inclined to suggest that Heaven is unique for each person.
We each can have our own personal Heavens, Hells, and
Purgatories.

In the moment of forming this, I chose to work towards my

future, yet that's extended life on Earth. I don't want to go to Heaven in the real world because I don't want to die to get there. I have, in my waking Earth life, seen multiple points of where Heaven exists on Earth and believe in perfect moments in our lives. We are allowed heavenly moments; moments of peace, and love, and togetherness. I don't want to die to leave people behind.

Because of death, I also wonder if that's why ghosts are a thing. There are definite boundaries between the living and the dead, yet I also want people to understand the forces of the not-yet-born. Linguistically, there is a cryptic message and meaning in that term, the not-yet-born.

When we read hyphenated words, it can mean they are primarily linked ideas that are connected, yet separate. We know that the word '*not*' implies that something isn't another, the word *yet* is the number 'one' in the Cantonese language, and *born* has a context of birthing children. Even if not in the concept of conception or birth, there is a premise.

A born-again Christian may be the next incarnation of a living person. Those who have not been reborn mix the term not-yet-born as a wish and curse for me. Some people may wish I be born again, yet at the same time, I'm alive on Earth, and I wish not to die to go to Heaven. I also urge that I can't fully grasp my admittance to Heaven or presume I'll be a father.

If there is a unified Heaven, then that realm is divine and explicitly the best things, people, and situations for all. I'd think that Heaven has a collective heart, desires, and soul, and my understanding of Heaven is a place where all people have their most fantastic wants and experiences manifest. It's a place where each other bolsters, strengthens and magnifies those wants and skills further. My version is an exponential and potentially infinite expansion of synergistic and divine unity, peacefulness, and bliss.

Heaven can be considered the ultimate best for *every* person, though on Earth, we're working together to allow each person their own divine experience. Singularly, as people, we have our likes and dislikes, though we remember the fact we're not the only people in existence. We can create our utopias, and guild with others who are building theirs, though it's the religious concept of Heaven that shuts off all other living things that might not fit into that mould.

Is that where Christianity would say that once we cut off all attachment to Earth, we go to Heaven? If that's true, I'm not entirely sure I'd like to do that because I still wish for a life on Earth to not be cut short. There are some fantastic people on Earth, and I wonder what would be different if we weren't here.

I've been pushing for meaning by attempting to be vital for those on Earth, yet is it that because my soul is urging for purpose so that I don't pass off into the afterlife? Are fear and concern about death and the afterlife what motivates me to keep pressing the keys assuring a continued life on Earth? We're told 'God's will be done,' and I'm not God; I'm a human holding my micro and macrocosmic wishes.

When it was 2:16 AM and I had a flash of happiness and truth confirmed by the sound of a message on my phone (Christy's email), I took it as a signal that life is on track, *and* I've been doing the correct things. Then, when I start writing and dive into my presumed ideas, I feel uncertain that my work has any meaning at all.

If my work is meant to impact the world, would I not be more successful and be aware of a positive effect from it? Or, is this part of the incubation process? It may be I'm to birth works and books to help those on Earth and the pieces of the puzzle that haven't lived yet.

I've also heard that time exists so that everything doesn't happen at once. We've been told things need time to occur, yet the Law of Attraction and some spiritual guides have promised miracles can happen instantaneously. Some show us too that time can be shifted, twisted and turned in our favour, so is that God giving the blessings, or is it the Universe? Where is the balance of control and allowing?

If science is right, then what is left to assist us towards the fact that every letter, word, message, and even video is a pact some have made to those living, dead, or not-yet-born? What about the links to Heaven and the afterlife and the direct connections from those angels like how Christy affects us? If Christy is a link to my divine network of people on Earth, and she and I are both linked to Heaven, then is it not the Global Organized Distractions that tell us when our paths have crossed?

The ways amaze the rays of a son that reminds his Dad that a Mother needs to stay on Earth to let her orbit with him around the sun. Each person values different things, yet if Universal concepts are valid and accurate for *all* people, then would that not apply to entities and attributes of the past, present, and future?

Some people have died and are guiding us and our future generations from a place physically separate. They may cognitively link our consciousness, yet these beings also may assure we need not pass off the mortal soil of Earth. If people are in Heaven, they might wish and hope we can have such wondrous lives as they have while staying here on Earth.

While those who've passed away may feel sad for leaving others behind, perhaps some in Heaven wish we were with them to love again and try to pull us through the ether to their afterlife. The living also can enjoy us so actively on Earth that others don't take us away from the living world.

Death may call for some to pass off and on, yet that can also be a motivation to live even more vigorously. We know some are afraid of dying, and yet others may desire to take their own life. People that have tried to commit suicide have failed with substantial reasons assuring they stay on Earth.

For me, when I slashed my wrist, I thought of my parents and how I don't want to leave them behind. For some others, they too might need to be reminded that there are some shards and shreds of purpose and meaning they need to share with Earth. Heaven can exist here, in the living realms for us, and I believe Christy helps the process so that we find perfect and divine moments in living life; she has done that for me.

Our awareness of the divine, while being a living conduit for it, instills hope, faith, and truth, and it's the reminder that we all are infinite beings that can bring Heaven to our lives. From the Lord's Prayer, I've gleaned meaning that the Kingdom of Heaven is meant to exist on Earth too, and though I can't comprehend the separate realms of the literal Heaven and Hell, it's my wish and prayer that others also may exist on Earth in a heavenly state.

I've seen the birds flying through the sky as if I was living in Heaven, and I've seen people walk up from the underworld as if from Hell. I am yet alive now. The wish, hope, and prayer are that I'll be active in the year 2053; live and saying Earth may be considered the middle ground.

Purgatory can separate everyone's deepest fears and most fantastic fantasies. The tipping point is when we realize that our intrinsic wants and truths reveal whether we pass from overdosing on life or enduring through time. I prefer to persist over time. Others too may find their insights into how to live like they are in Heaven while still alive on Earth.

Thank you, Christy! You've helped me find a purpose statement! I was online and heard my phone 'bling,' and it was your email. I read the email and then thought to write my thanks and response to the question "do you think creating Heaven on Earth is possible?"

Christy has been an exceptional online mentor for me for a few years now, and this chapter is a slightly modified version of the email I wrote that night. My previous depth of purpose was "to provide." The clarified message is that I want to provide Heaven to those alive while they are on Earth.

Helping people with food, water, and shelter is an objective, yet I also want to give hopes, goals, love, and dreams. I may not yet know the point in time where I pass off from the realms of the living, yet if I'm isolated and alone at the computer, can I still share? Yes.

Are writing books and emails a pathway to allowing people to like and love their lives? I don't know. Will others even read this? I hope, yes. Christy's message planted these seeds.

After the video:

After hearing what Christy and Martin Rutte shared, I recalled Christy is Italian. *Molto grazie* means thank you very much, or more specifically many graces. The response *prego* is *I pray*.

If we agree that Heaven is a state of being and that we all can have access and grant other people's Heaven on Earth, then I'm reminded to breathe. Rewind to the question, "Do you think creating Heaven on Earth is possible?" I don't think we can *create* it, though we can positively assure we *allow* it to thrive.

We also can choose and create things that infuse elements of what allows others and ourselves more heavenly moments. I liked how Martin talks about how the Torah didn't have a translation of a one-way departure from the Garden of Eden. It reminded me, as they both said, how people can choose to be or live in heavenly ways or states of being.

The word 'amazing' also trips in here how we can know the entire pathway of the maze and go back into the labyrinth to help bring people through to Heaven again. The idea of life being a maze alludes to an intuition; forces have found divine bliss and freedom to help others lost reach their places of joy and happiness.

Some rooms in the maze may be filled with sadness or chaos, though, and if we can bring each person into alignment and allyment, we may find common ground of peace, love, unity, and respect.

With feelings and emotions, there's a saying: "That that carves deep into the heart with sadness can only be again filled with joy." What then of those that have been through Hell on Earth that can help guide and direct people back to Heaven on Earth?

In my 'before' comments, I didn't recall to mention the credo or prerogative of PLU8R. Although maybe not a total solution of Heaven on Earth, if we can activate global PLUR, we'll be moving a lot closer to a cohesive experience. Global

PLUR is Peace in every nation, Love for every race, Unity of every creed, and Respect for every religion.

The concept can be a compass of sorts, yet also is intrinsic as a value system. From the before part too, if a religious or spiritual realm of Heaven is separate from the existing domain we're in, then those who have passed onto Heaven may be those guides nudging or drawing us through the maze of Earth towards them.

Some people (yes, like me) want to stay trapped in the labyrinth and also want to help people find their rooms of eternal happiness. I may have teetered on the edges of being sent to the afterlife, yet as I sit here at home isolated and profoundly aware, I don't want to think about the concept of a religious or spiritual war.

I remind us of an idea about the word *aware* and its potential hyphenation; *a-war-e*. When we are an extra of war, we may not be on the main stage or in battle, yet our consciousness is still pervading. Or, if the religious texts are right and the war is already won, then how can we heal the world and reverse the damage done to the lives, societies, and wellbeing of Mother Earth? Can we remedy and assure another war need not occur?

There are battles and conflict in the world, and if each person upheld, expanded, and strengthened bonds of PLUR and PLU8R as a responsibility (the second R of PLU8R), maybe the concept of a full representation of Heaven on Earth will more justly manifest.

If our world of Earth is just one tiny planet in an entire cosmos of time, space, and matter (recalling in the $E=MC^2$ equation the speed of light (instant miracles)) then maybe another soul might not need to wait 16 billion years only to reach Heaven on Earth.

What if there are alien or extraterrestrial beings that have an alternate concept of what Heaven is? Is Heaven a human concept, or is there a universal version of Heaven? If we are alive, we are conscious, and we may choose how we act, react, or respond. If we are aware and not an extra of war, does that mean we must battle? What if Heaven is a Kingdom and Earth is one of its subjects locked in orbit around a star that was colonized by a single thought?

What if we on Earth are just a dream in the minds of another being and are purely immaterial and just kicked like a pebble into the cosmic dance of life? What if they discovered our planet and are using us as a petri dish to see how our cultures intermingle like sands through the hourglass? Or, if we take a solipistic perspective, how can we assure that we live another day if we feel we're ready for Heaven?

I hope I am ready for Heaven, just that I need not fall into the hands of Death to reach it. It's a bold choice for some to choose life and the betterment of the world of Earth; not in comparison to other planets or even other people, yet instead, our journeys of self-discovery and empowerment guiding, nurturing, and tending the seeds of hope, love, and prosperity.

We increase the chances of others to remain on Earth and find their versions of Heaven while alive. Thank you, Christy, for the link. I appreciate you, your friends, family, network, and followers for helping me with this. It may be unclear and a joke that few get, yet thank you for reminding us that we can have it all, that we always have had it all.

Though, if we're not right enough with ourselves, and the world, to allow ourselves Heaven on Earth, we must reconnect it with life. Ti amo! Io sono un pazo per voi!

I MUST TELL YOU TOO

I'm learning how to walk my talk, and some of my text shares God's words and works. I'm also quite Earthy, so am not seeking to land in Heaven.

Like I typed in Christy's chapter, I believe we can find Heaven on Earth and hope we draw some people out of their Earth-Hells. I've understood and accepted, I'm a vassal, and as I have climbed from the pit before, there are crisp reminders that cling to my being.

We don't earn Salvation, yet in gratitude, we receive it. I'm compelled to share works and words in ways that shall call others to navigate through our Heavenly maze. I again, though, explore the night with depths of my devotion. I recommend an essential book by Jack Canfield called *The Success Principles*.

I had edited the first chapter of *Fragments of Intent* the night I bought Jack's book for a friend. Earlier in the day, I had manually revised the second chapter of *Etched in Stone* and was split between works like an A.D.D. thing. I appreciate being able to break between projects when I reach a wall, though, when I wrote this part, Nat's beauty was radiating through my smile.

Smiles keep the tears wept kept in a flask, and I remembered to get Lewis Howes' book *The Mask of Masculinity*. I've neglected to pursue some of the urges of my heart, and though my recordings are still part of the process, a unique twisted idea in my thoughts is that my music shall expand. I've said I'm 'cart before the horse' person sometimes and it implies how my books are where I'm the workhorse, and my tracks are what I should be carrying.

Perhaps God siphons and ciphers my tracks while the books hold His ideas to the foundations to stay in place.

"Cycling parameters spin to a sphere because a linear direction is all that you hear."

Time is a one-way linear form, and the premise is the recordings are made and also etched in stone as pieces of time; rhymes that God uses for me to build. Do we still construct and find future homes for others and ourselves?

The recording on the stereo at this point was *Stolen Thought*. It alluded that Natalie's the boss and I'm the vassal performing work for *her* world, even if she and I are not to be a couple. There are so many weird and unusual twists that seem to urge me into belief while surging me forward with a release and relief; it's a choice we make.

The pathway leads up to the door of the home. The garden on the left holds the pond outside the master bedroom, and the glass walls on either side of the house allow those inside to see out. Perhaps the two-way directivity of glass needs to be protected as the vaulted ceilings above the pit hold two ceiling fans that keep the air moving.

In the home, the wall case of books in the main office stems from the first vision I saw of the house. The shelves hold five hundred books that I've read while the desktop is extensive with a corkboard on the wall behind. Photos of my family and our travels are pinned up to remind me of our fun and love.

We host visitors twenty to thirty times a year, though these visitors gather to work on their relationships, businesses, and creative projects. With the support of my wife and myself, two to three-day visits with those we've met gather, and we've met these people on our travels. Some are other friends that find their way from different parts of Earth.

The home is safe and secure and located in Australia. Providing Point was my commitment in 2018, though I hadn't gathered the community together with my intents to provide. There is some money going to Chilliwack from the book sales, yet I could not solve the situation as I'd intended on my own.

In July 2018, I accepted my meanders around points of place and time. My work wasn't yet cemented firm and fettered to faith, yet instead, my heart needed to be tethered to fate and be free. Visions tracked around the spools of CDs hold my being as I saw I'd been pushing for the purpose. I wanted to provide instead of sharing love more truly with people that reciprocate care.

I found my way to earning another car, Colin helped me get the floor plans ready, and in 2024, the home's construction began. I remembered to heed my instincts and intuitions, and like how Taylor reminded me to focus thought upon what I want, I told myself to not push *for* purpose, yet rather to *have* meaning and use.

The Fountains seemed not to be providing the waters of life, yet perhaps it was because the glaciers needed to melt to give them their vital energy. I commit to the process again and again, and with the thread of this work coursing into my purpose driven promises, we meet the completion of *The Fountains of Fortitude*.

Fortitude is a tricky thing and subject; the consequences of decades are substantial, yet only fragments of eternity. I wish to wield and yield millennia into the space of one rhyme, yet the ladder may have been up against the wrong wall.

I couldn't return my gratitude of being given what I've received immediately. It took a few years since the first Fountain called my whims and wants into the dominoes of our consecration — each grain of sand from yesterday fuels how the sand had yet to be silt.

Home is a place to connect a loved idea. A car wasn't fair for me to have at the point of no regular job and no books sales, yet as my audience expands, it results in a just situation.

Two thousand two hundred four miles to go before landing and picking up a carton at Duty-Free. 40k feet in the air right now.
Resurfacing are some codal activities too. We develop the card types for people such as how artifacts are kind, fresh, and vital, and there are reminders to value them more for who they are as people. With contialitic function starting, we contact love and heart and can call the Khan or Shard truth.

Though it may not make sense, be absolute with *have to do* orders and operations. 4:15 is the destination. I took my meds, psychosis sucks, and we keep our health and strengthen the plucks.

This work drifted into the moments of rhyme. I chose to adjust my path to refuse music in a different way and definition. During the 2018 Festivus trip, my recordings seemed to seep out of my consciousness into the mental and visual fabric. Tapestries of the skies hold the glowing orbs, yet they also keep my soul.

I've been a chemical addict pressing the keys and boundaries of ability and permission, yet I may have returned to burning through the night. It was July 16th, 2018. Kyle and I agreed that I'd adopt Zeus.

There may be only one more chapter remaining in *Open to Fate*, yet creations stem. I give my heart, and I ask for a return. Please let us gather around the fire again in 2019 and find the threads wound from the sound.

A digital stitch puts my thoughts back on the Internet. It may be I sandwich my work; Much music as the bread, the books as the middle, though I'm not clear how *my* music is a layer of nourishment. I tend to think human interaction is the other slice of bread.

Regarding the Sprites, let them fly free. The Sprites may need us to find our ways to navigate through the shared maze, yet this is meant to twist into how the shards hold fragments of their own. Starbucks? Honour and respect the baristas and shops fully. Keep from overloading people with work and be active in connection to form a PLU8R inversion into the conversion of text.

The revision and restructuring of the Fountains are solid ideas concerned about the used and refused edits. If some say that promises from God more than a decade ago *are* part of His plan, then I shall relish and relevate in the luxury of allowing fate to occur. Messages from decades ago assist the web of time wrapping around sound.

The dreams from when we were children are still unfolding

into the magnification of our most profound wants of love. I'm not God, so I don't know so much about all the secrets of the Universe. I do, though, remind myself that God directs us by using my writing and recording to tell me what the truth is.

There is a drastic difference in who I am since when I started this sentence from when I heard the first look. The tasted intuition found tuition of the fission and fusion from *Hold the Bond*. What is the next chapter I edit?

The contraceptive moments of rhyme have been preventing some seeds from slipping into the felt tip. Chip the mp3 to cue me up to sup, and tell me secrets of love's circles and punctuation of the pup.

Scattered games find alphabetic names of wisdom and direct guidance, and it seems more natural to plow the fields of text at night alone. What of the harvests when people gather as a collective and then sell the wares at the market?

For those that help sell the books, thank you, though how shall you be compensated? As my books gather earnings as seeds that we may share in the gardens, this strews through the starship from a familial drip. Would a kind tip be what she wishes for to open the core?

A pause of time may not reverse, yet as we disperse *The Sands of Yesterday* out into the world, a curled up kitten shares the written for how I've bitten the line. I take in a sign that makes the spine trine up three points to one. The vinyl spun, yet I'm not The Son who you accused me of being.

I'm me, one who's set to see the ocean meet the glee and joy of the eyes of my baby boy. She toys with the web of the modes of text, and if you think of a small case 't,' then see how that letter is a cross. Even those who are an atheist, agnostic, or have a non-Christian religion, most of them know that the cross signifies Christ. With the words 'the truth,' see how the word *the* can separate to *t-he*. It's a word of the cross and the male pronoun 'he' without space. It's a definite article to note, and I add that it's a small H.

If we add spaces to different words, shards of language start to confuse and clarify. I want to assure the cross is a part of the world, yet if I start at the top and drop down to the bottom, think of adding 'L' for love into The Word, and you have The World.

"From the left, right, front, back, back into the mainframe. Program selected name."

The Glass House has kept me up at night. I couldn't sleep one night because I was envisioning the home, so I went to the computer to write more in this book. Returning, though, I found the cryptic and caustic beverage in the same cup from which I drink.

I'm inclined to write more at night, yet the chemicals contaminate. There is a drastic pull between thinking healthy choices are what my heart desires, and a belief about substances is crucial to my creative development. Am I condensing time's crystals and compressing my future timelines with drugs?

The Healing Hearts version of *Fragments of Intent* wasn't done yet, though my recordings are part of this. I'm approaching two decades of music as well as my written work without many sales. My books are only two to three years old, yet they may still expand. Both crafts hold an evolution of ability, though what shall be the third strand to braid them together?

Julianna talked to me and told me that although we may not know the next steps, it's best to keep open to ideas and opportunity. Though we don't know what the future holds, we also must have faith we'll find our next steps. My work is what I must nurture and nourish, though my concern is the chemicals are parenting this work.

I didn't have a job in the previous two years, though I planted some seeds in the community and cosmos. My faith chains me to the present moment as I tended to blame God for what happens when I don't understand. Some psychologists would accuse us of creating our unknown selves, and there are parts of myself that expose and embarrass me without a conscious reaction or comprehension.

I have an idea that a lot of what I know as absolutes may not yet be perceived, and my fears have tried to gnaw into my psyche. Subtle allusions of death creep into consciousness eluding my forgotten stone — the stability of my faith waivers from nil to repentant energy and attitude with defiant wishes to thrive.

I best not defy God. He knows me better than I could ever tell another. Fragments of my mind siphon a lost potion of denial, yet I shift to urge the smiles not to struggle. There is despair woven in the thread, yet we almost all recall the walls that hold many in, and almost everyone out.

I don't want to be defiant or dismissive as I yearn and wish to thrive. I have sometimes refused to submit to the displayed results formed as we've not gathered even up to ten patrons for Providing Point. I thought my books would be an income source to house people, yet less than twenty books have sold on Amazon as of May 2019.

I wonder if you see these shifts in my writing; from fantastic faith to the fears of a fatalistic wraith. I twist between believing all things are possible to think there is no other possible way. Deterministic belief in fate, to again wondering if it's even worth it for me to create.

I've met a point in my bookwork where I trust the process of typing and revising and refining. I wonder if I just grind away for our needs and goodness to come from what I've written. Is it delusion or sheer determination that allows destiny to hold the plow?

I wonder if it's because I refuse to understand that I still need to tell you. I'm not a saviour or Christ, and I'm paranoid people want to end my life for not believing in or proclaiming religious or spiritual ideas. I wonder if death has been hounding me and pushing messages into my awareness that Earth doesn't want me here.

If Earth doesn't want me here, I'm not a righteous or holy person that wants to go to Heaven. I don't wish to go to Hell either, though maybe it's then again how I'm a coward for not wanting to go to war. I'm afraid of calling myself good because I don't want to fight.

Is that how this book is *Open to Fate*? I open a moment to look into my lack of understanding and comprehension; I reveal a willingness to surge dreams to provide and do something that changes the course of events on Earth. I *am* only one person, and since I'm not God or have magical powers, I also remind myself of the will of all that's drastically beyond the influence of my waning heart.

I seem not to have praised God, though am meekly thankful that I'm allowed to live and be. Perhaps there is repentance to be made for how this world develops. I seem to think reparations must prepare many sources of life that are part of the next Fountain's journey.

WHAT'S YOUR BIG IDEA?

Even if we can't actualize our own big idea, I think each person should have one. If you do have a fantastic concept, put it on paper or into a file and share it with someone! That's what this chapter is for me.

Introversial and Providing Point are two of my seeds. I've not tended or activated them correctly, though I want to tell you the ideas and how they expand to share a vision. Big ideas can affect Earth, and people make things. Some of those people also are givers and wish to help. Providing Point is my big idea, though Introversial is a small branch of it.

Introversial is using Patreon, a crowdfunding site, to gather pledges for providing locally on street level. The premise and promise of Providing Point are to provide food, shelter, and water for people. The broader concept is to provide for *all* people and should not be limited just to the town I live in. It is, I think, a potentially transferrable idea for other creators.

My work includes premises I've gleaned from online mentors such as giving part of my book and music earnings. From a Gary Vaynerchuk principle of giving 51%/49% to Lewis Howes conveying the idea of providing something to a massive number of people; in his case to inspire people 100 million people to earn a full-time income doing what they love. I learned from Water.org that near one billion people don't yet have access to clean and safe water, and Christy Whitman seeded the idea that we are unlimited and can achieve anything. Jack Canfield teaches the principles of how to succeed, though I mixed all these ideas up, and on August 2nd, 2018 made another shift and pivot.

Providing Point's Introversial branch is a gathering point where I share my books and music, though it is meant to, at this point, offer grocery cards to people. All earned (after

Patreon and PayPal fees) through Introversial's Patreon page goes to others for Share and Care cards as of July 2018. I give digital books and music as rewards for pledging, though I've not pushed firmly enough for pledges up to now. I don't like mooching money, so had believed I could entice people to contribute because of access to the books.

There is a multi-win if the Patreon earnings go to others. If people want to contribute to the cause, their generosity provides efficiently, and patrons also receive books and music as a reward. By sharing printed copies of the books, we also can share the ideas of Providing Point and expand through readership.

Ideas proliferate. As part of the books' sales earnings also go to various charities, the more people purchasing books also allows us to provide more to the causes. The more earned through Patreon also allows additional viewership, and if people choose to read or play the reward items, they can help involute the work outwards.

If others made their work and commitment to providing for people in their local communities, there could be other Providing Points in other cities and towns, and if other creators pledge part of their earnings or provide their work and art to Providing Point patrons, we can offer more.

Providing Points in other communities can work for different causes, and gatherers can work with other artists, authors, and musicians to share their material with patrons. Though Providing Point is the overarching program and name, it's not yet so much of a legally bound non-profit. We've not gathered enough to register governmentally.

As of May 2019, Introversial's Providing Point is 7x patrons and me. I'm working to find a Shared Freedom Solution as a concept to ensure we take care of all people. Dan Holguin's advice about weight loss being one pound at a time, then for gathering and providing, one person at a time. What I must give too is genuine love and care.

Would other people want to glean from creators sharing their work via Providing Points? It may be a mutual benefit.

If we can gather more creative work and share it for pledges, creators can expand their audience. We may assemble and collect more creators and contributors, and we can share and provide a more diverse catalogue of creative works for patrons.

If we can encourage more pledges, we can expand our reach via patrons, and an increase in the potential audience for artistic contributions can lead to additional exposure and support for creators. If we can increase the number of people who know about the artists, the artists may sell more of their work, and the causes they work for shall glean more awareness and earnings via patronship.

What would happen if different Providing Point gatherers found creators who could provide an overvalued offer for patronship? If we could provide twenty or thirty dollars of value in creative work monthly for pledges (instead of my infrequent Fountain releases), there would be additional motivations for commitments to give instead of marketing only the causes.

When in my creative process and understanding, I shift my commitments, and I restate some premises and promises. As of August 3rd, 2018, I committed to sharing 100% of the individual Fountains earnings to different causes and charities. If part of my work's profits goes to various purposes, I think we can do more in the form of giving.

I want to help the homeless and low-income people in town, though I'd also like to share with others who need or want support too; part of my cause is improving Earth and not just the Fraser Valley. Similar to the chapter *Buckle Up Koyich* in the 6th Fountain, I must share my promises.

I have gotten edgy, insecure, and nervous when I reach these points of commitment, yet keep at it. I know I'm doing good work, and I remind myself of some of the concepts I believe. I push past with faith that we have gotten this far into the process of the Fountains books.

My obsessive compulsion carries a lot of this too. I know if we earn sales and gain patrons I'd feel more fulfilled, and I've sometimes felt stagnant and believed I'm wasting my time, effort, and energy. I keep writing because I like the work, and, even if it's not rational, I believe I can earn for myself too.

I repent for not activating Providing Point in Chilliwack to success yet as of May 2019. I've not wanted to mooch money or pledges, and I've not marketed my books and music well up to now. I've lacked drive, ambition, and the motivation required, and I also must atone for not being active on street level getting to know more people.

I need to reach out more frequently to people, and I've been a star-crossed waffle who's dealing with my own mental health issues and recovery. Since this is the closing chapter of the eighth Fountain and you may not have read previous ones, I want to condense and summarize the Fountains up to now.

I started the first Fountain book, *Finding Natalie,* wishing to share the book with the world so that Natalie Imbruglia would come and meet me. I intended on writing the entire book from her perspective, yet fell from that after the first chapter. I picked up voices of a few other people in the second chapter and then wrote outwards to her and the world of Earth. The book included one chapter written to Chandra, though she didn't want it to be public.

The second Fountain book, *Searching for Tomorrow* was me starting to think about what I was going to do if I didn't meet Natalie. I started plotting and planning and using gimmicky marketing tactics with the intent to earn money through writing. I included a chapter written to Gary Vaynerchuk at the close of the book, as he was my primary guidepost at that time with online learning. It also was part of my process in developing proficient authorship even if the book too was awfully written.

From the Valley to the Fountain started with the remembrance of my first believed love, the Original Lovestone; Althea Rae Megas. I shared thoughts about my chemical habits and also a bit about my tainted past. I wrote the book trying to push my purpose and dreams, and though the Natalie dream wasn't as prominent, perhaps I am stubborn as a mule and free as a lark as one chapter said.

I combined the first three Fountains book into a compilation titled *Fragments of Intent*. It was the first substantial book that I released as the first three individual Fountains were training grounds for learning how to write and publish. The manuscript went through some drastic revision and the final version re-released in October 2018. Two-thirds of the 3rd Fountain didn't reach the completed version, and the first three Fountains are not available individually.

It was the three-part book *The Sands of Yesterday* where we started to grip in. Although I had the idea of the Seed Fund when writing the 3rd Fountain, the 4th, 5th, and 6th Fountains honed my craft and started to germinate my faith. I released a few different versions of the books as I learned how to edit, revise, and improve my writings. Although the Unlimited texts formed individually, the books now have gathered into their current available and final forms. The post-Unlimited copies bundled into *The Sands of Yesterday,* and the last revision resulted in the Sanctified Spirit version of that three-part book.

The 7th Fountain, *Etched in Stone*, is the Fountain before this one. It's also now in a post-Unlimited form and started the three Fountains of Fortitude which are this book, *Shards of my Soul.* The version you see now is how I've allowed myself to become as I put wishes out of the Universe to guide me and let me heed the forces of Heaven and Hell. I also open my control to the hands of Fate.

Other authors also don't always know whom they channel, and that's part of my mystery too. I think I wrote this, yet I know I didn't do so entirely by myself. By the point this text reaches you, it's gone through multiple distillations changing into this sequence and series of words.

But what is the core of my big idea? I've thought to earn, gather, and share abundance. I have wanted to provide for others and myself when it's been I who's been in lack. How can I make enough money to afford a basic living wage for myself, let alone a thousand other people? How can I wish and decree Providing Point could house the entire population of homeless in the Fraser Valley when we only have $46 pledged?

I believe the forces of fate and destiny use me as a conduit for global significance even if I'm isolated and alone most of the time. I understand there are higher powers that have massive reach and have believed they are secretly conspiring to allow me to thrive instead of smiting me for being a dramatically flawed human.

During Christmas 2017, I believed Earth was going to be destroyed. I'd also thought the one I fell for in 1998 had wished me to be dead to meet her in Heaven. If Zeus is angry that Jesus took over the role of a primary person to be worshiped, then how have I been so daft not even to speak that I too believe in God and pray to Him?

I've been allowed to exist here in moments of radical thankfulness to be alive, and I've believed I'm not a standard human suited to live in society. If I can find such happiness and feelings of intense love for others when I'm isolated and alone, imagine what I could do for a real lovestone that loves me in return?

Why haven't I shown appreciation and spoken up to ask a real girl for a dance? If Natalie wasn't my soulmate, then why am I still thinking of her twenty years later while believing she wishes I knew the truth?

"I still don't know."

I don't want to close this with declarations and wishes for the future. I also don't want to make claims of false truth or audacious accusations. I'd like to know how these books are valuable to people even if they aren't a commercial success, and I'd adore and love to know if Providing Point is an idea to pursue or if I should release it as unsuccessful. What is my purpose, and what can I do to share and feel real love?

I've been working towards a living legacy, yet I feel like I have so few to speak with and that people are avoiding me. The cat is fantastic, and I like that he's here, so perhaps that's part of this. My spiritual comprehension and parental influences also remind me I have work to perform. If I want to have a life of prosperity and abundance, it won't always magically happen. There are miracles; Zeus is right of that. I also now know I learn to live *with* someone, not merely *for* them.

A selfless attitude and ethics are neat things, though many others have also told me they think I should work entirely for just my benefit and earnings. Gratefulness and reciprocation allure me into moments to play and pray, and when working on my projects, I've found disturbingly good moments of clarity. My obsessions remind me what is right, at least for me.

I don't know what's best for others, though. I continue to thrive, create, and give, though I also must not do good things just so that good things happen to me.

"The right thing, at the right time, for the right reason."-Owen Beattie

I must also add *to and for the right people.*

(Here is the close of the 8th Fountain)

163

RESPONSIBILITY

Three weeks before this book started, Zeus moved into my home. Zeus doesn't speak English, he wants me to play more than I do, and I feel sad that I've not been fantastic for him so much yet. I remind us, Zeus is my cat.

Commitments and promises are a strange twist. We may make promises to do things, and when locked into commitments, we also have a responsibility. The fear I have is I may not be there yet regarding previous obligations, yet here we are we're here. Bookwork has me alone sometimes, and though a semi-frequent occurrence, I've been focused on my work again.

Each of us is *not* entirely set apart from reality, many of us bridge and bond metapsychically, and I wonder if it's easier not to disappoint people and stay committed to tending home? Home is where we cannot only feel love, though also live with respect. Although Zeus may expect more from me than I've yet provided, I hope he knows I'm working for a combined future; not just our own.

Our home is Earth, and my apartment is a place for us to reside. Adventures out of the house help remove the feeling that home is just a comfortable prison, though with Zeus locked up here, he may feel like he's a prisoner. When Zeus first moved here, I thought he was trying to make me *his* prisoner.

When I started this Fountain, chains of addiction were still haunting. Up to the point of writing this, the shambled embers of cigarettes helped weave the loom. It's almost like Voldemort when I think about specific people, and even if I may wish to never interact with them, do they want me gone? Is it a delusion or paranoia that calls my fear?

Differently, Mom was to visit soon. I hope Mom becomes

more appreciated for the beautiful human she is. It's not comfortable being human, let alone being responsible as a parent, and though it's not so comfortable being alone, having some love helps. Like a cat, I can be solitary, yet I need love and contact too.

When I have so much to say and have no one to talk to, I wish I could converse with my cat. If cats honestly can't speak English, it may feel like no one understands when all we hear is 'meow.' Zeus helps me learn who I am and what we think, even if I wish he could talk.

I try to comprehend what it's like to be another, sometimes. When there's no potential for understanding, some preach forgiveness and acceptance, yet there must be more we can do. I may neglect or over focus, and working with these books, it can be helpful and worthwhile to take a break.

Zeus was crunching on his kibble when I started this book. We didn't have much to eat at home at that point, yet we receive appreciated support. I want to pick up my cat and squeeze and snuggle all the feelings of love and life into him, and though not my human child, our fur babies can help teach us to be parents.

Is it easier to leave some alone and give up? It could be. If another gives up on us, then they don't have to live with or tend to us through the years. We can't always find ways to show how and with what we're okay, and sometimes I'm *not* okay. Are you alright?

It was not a comfortable place in July 2018, though at least I had a home. On August 8th, 2018, this Fountain's pages began, and I felt like I should be taken away from the world; curled up into isolation so I can write and work. I didn't have a girlfriend, and I indeed didn't have so many beautiful things to say or share.

I was in a poor me state for a few months, and my faith knows that's not the right way to live. I've sometimes been low and solemn, though when I'm writing, I look towards the future and hope to build a fantastic one. I can't imagine it yet.

Even when I've been pissed off or depressed, I live a pretty good life. Zeus and I shall hopefully be in the same home for a few years, and a learned autonomy comes through living alone. I hadn't lived with anyone for seven to eight years, and it was only in July 2018 that Zeus moved in.

Some people know how to live alone, though knowing love is out there can slow a mind to a stop. Our life is for others, ourselves, and also for the world, though some of us may want to be alone. We can be alone *without* lacking love, though, and a cat is a fortunate connection to have.

Pets are someone to squiggle out all our positive feelings of affection and kindness, though the way some are about touch, physical contact isn't always appreciated. Two ways to show love is through gifts and also physical touch, though I need to learn how to convey heart and happiness in other ways too.

Some of our homes are places for people to gather, and when friends have visited, Zeus has hidden away. He could be part of the interactions, and it seems I'm in real training grounds to prepare to raise a live human being. When I don't understand what Zeus is saying, or he doesn't talk, I can still aim to be loving and kind and communicate.

We can pick up people's spirits by giving a kind word, and some people appreciate it when we offer time or service; that's a way of providing love also. Making the time and effort to connect can be helpful to build relationships if another is sad or depressed, and some people just need a friend. If we only connect because we have to, though, and not because we feel happy to do so, it may not always be right.

Differently, when we do things only because we want to and not because the other wants it, it's not always a win for either. We can tell. We need to find more ways to interact with people that mutually benefit us and are a shared desire.

Giving someone alone or focus time is a thing to be appreciated because some people value solitude. I'm thankful to have the time to write these books and thank many for allowing me to communicate with Earth. I also thank you for forgiving me for being a self-focused and obsessed human.

Just because I don't want to interact with someone or love

to connect with them, though, it doesn't mean they're an adversary. I best be cautious, though, because I've been awful at showing correct attention and contact sometimes. I know we're not necessarily intended for everyone. I'm not against some, though prefer less contact, and I hope to learn how to interact and tell people that correctly.

Social issues are quite pervasive; we're on Earth, and there are a lot of humans on this planet. Going through depression, some may feel useless and unappreciated, yet each of us is one of the most crucial pieces of our life. Without living and being through our years, there would be no us. I may need to work, think, and process what I'd like to do, and I also need to learn how to care and not just earn for the future.

Some people need full attention when another is with them, and it's a good thing to give. Paying attention to people is a way to offer kindness, and though living alone teaches autonomy, I'm keenly aware I may need contact to be okay. We *can* build an extraordinary life if we want it, and my mind seems to tell me we do that. I mustn't give away my entire being and attention to only one person, though.

I hope people learn to accept you. I know we each may be flawed beings who need to get past our issues, yet the other part of being human is we can choose to shut out everyone and everything. We may do what we think we need to do, yet the hope is we also may grant and receive grace, connection, and kindness.

And for the others who'll read this; you may have a few things to say too. As I continue to learn how to work and play, I hope we can also learn to care and cherish more. I'd like to know when it's okay to give someone a hug or an honest compliment and determine truth like a cat. I know it's a bit creepy to brush past someone's legs to say hello, though.

This Fountain is also about my goals, hopes, and dreams too and uses the R-Words from the PLU8R philosophy. PLUR (without an 8) is peace, love, unity, and respect, though the version with an eight includes many other R-words.

There are people in our lives that focus on letting our

dreams come true, and my responsibility is to help tend the seeds and soil. Zeus is an essential and primary relationship in my daily living life, and my Mom and my Dad are also both vital to my work, my process, and me. Parents can be crucial and miss teaching us critical lessons, though. Mine may not have explained or told me how to think when I was younger, and some of what I learn comes from intuition and my mistakes. I showed up here on Earth as my parent's son without knowing we'd have the lives we have.

My cat and I are living at home, and I don't smoke inside anymore. I wish and hope we'll always have food, water, and a place to live, though I may like to gain some more things like a girlfriend and a car. We learn and process a lot of stuff some humans may never comprehend.

Codes, information, and podcasts teach about high-level humans, and with more time to play, Zeus and I can learn to love and thrive more than we yet understand. Physical affection teaches us about intuitive communication, and if you ever picked up and snuggled your pet, you know what love can be. With humans too, we can respond more often to the calls of our heart and lean into trust, and even if I've not had a girlfriend in a few years, I learn to think more about others than myself.

I must remember not to be selfish and think only about what I want. Temptations of pleasure may lure, and though cigarettes were part of my life when I started writing this book, I keep them on the patio. My experience may not be so majestic at this point, yet I'm happy and thankful to have a home and also grateful and fortunate to live.

As winter arrived, I wished all people could have a place to live where they don't have to worry about the cold. On Zeus' third night here in July, voices and visions of his previous home coursed through my mind. I heard the sounds of his previous owners and thoughts about their other cat. I don't know how much Zeus misses them, though it's a goal to make sure both of us are glad, thankful, and happy to live here even if it's not always been easy.

A waterfall of relief flows over my mind and body. The imagined feeling carries a layer of hope over my soul that earns us a life beyond our current level of existence. I hope we meet at The Glass House and that we'll also be able to thrive and go adventuring. Many wish and want an abundant life and prosperity and search for their freedoms. Let life grant us each what we want to have and do.

I intend to be patient about liberty and happiness, and its fate that landed us here. The thing is, we know where we are now, and we need to know and accept our current situation. We also need to know where we want to be. Held here in this apartment, I may not yet appreciate or envision all of how grand life can and shall be, yet we move into the future moments together.

I'm aware I've committed my life to you as well as the ones that I love. There are reasons for me to become more recluse and spend a lot of time at home, and if my beliefs are correct, then we may find some useful things and energy. My ideas include some psychotic and potential delusions, like a belief in telepathy, though if you are alive and understand life, you know some many secrets of your own.

Privy only to cats and their feline friends, some thoughts are a profound thing. We can grant great things, ideas, and activities, and when entertaining thoughts and cats, we may sense the spirits directed at us sometimes. I must remember that cats are often our protectors while Zeus has his own issues to deal with. I refract myself while processing the document I share with you.

Thank you for reading into my thoughts as we work through performing this for a beautiful, happy, and prosperous future. Many humans may think I'm entirely delusional, yet I consider some of what I believe matters. I remind us that cats domesticated us, not the other way around as we each hold secrets and truths about life on Earth, even if we don't agree.

I may not yet have a life where my pets can play in the woods and chase all the creature of the forest, yet dreams keep us open to the future. Envision *your* life the way you'd like it and work towards that vision. About the people you interact with, please introduce them to new people too.

This book formed by the sands of time; printed and written with a kitten's guidance. It tells us how some of you may not yet have met, yet this fountain includes chapters sourced by different people who matter a lot. We share messages that we need to know; like how this chapter was directed to Zeus and then revised for a broad audience.

Who reads this book? I don't know yet. Some people know who *you* are, yet may not understand who you live with. However, our journeys evolve thought, emotion, and psychic guidance, because as we're all connected, the lines are redirected and reflected by our minds.

The Medallion group are three people that have shown significant amounts of love, connection, and kindness. I don't mention their real names, yet they're three primary people who have been very generous with food, drink, resources, and a shared connection. I've not written chapters to them yet, though some beings remind us in the keenest sense that love is what matters.

Working to earn respect and money is a thing, and as we may need to allow it, love can be there the entire time. If I'm too focused on my work or other words, though, I may neglect love; I know I certainly have sometimes.

Many blessings of truth, patience, and connection travel to you as I thank you for letting us continue. For the next few years, I may try not to control others or cater to them with guilt, though there is a law of permission and allowance.

It's best we learn how and what to communicate about what we want and don't want. PLUR; Peace, Love, Unity, and Respect. We remind the threads to wind about the loom.

REPRESENTATION

I wrote this section the night after writing the previous. I'd said something that day that caused my Mom sadness. I called myself a piece of shit. I had been feeling very cynical and angry and wasn't happy with the cat living here, and I was not pleased with myself. The first five to six weeks of living with Zeus was a difficult adjustment.

I believe in PLU8R as a high value. Respect is the first R of PLU8R, though this chapter is Representation. It may not be rational to think of a cat being able to understand when we talk, though I believe they can. Reciprocation and representation are universal principles, and I felt frustrated, controlled, and angry. I considered letting Zeus go to a different home.

I don't like abandoning commitments, though, and a layer of shame and defiance blended. My confidence in my mental health was awful when I first wrote this, and Zeus had compounded my dissatisfaction with life. I thought about releasing the cat to a home where love may be more pervasive.

My desire and need for autonomy run far too high for my liking. I don't like how I refuse to set myself aside sometimes, and I've not tended so well to the lives and hearts of others. Working on books is a singular focus, and when feeling the cat's demanding attention, it's difficult; especially since we can't have a conversation.

Zeus is a fantastic and active cat, and adapting to him was entirely a 'me' issue. I thought I needed to sacrifice myself entirely for him and live solely for his benefit, though too much self-sacrifice can build resentment. Resentment is not an R of PLU8R.

Mom was going through issues of her own, and though I couldn't be right there to hug her and squeeze a ton of love, affection, and wishes of hope into her, I remind us we do love.

I thank Mom for being a fantastic mother, and I felt sad about how tearful she sounded when I demeaned myself.

Empathy is what lures me to keep afloat, though. As I learn how to love, sanity helps keep me together. I need to learn how to bridge and bond with genuine connection and acceptance, and I also told my Mom: "I've been through worse, and I shall be through better." She called it false optimism, yet that's because she didn't believe *I* thought it was true.

We can't always assure what the future holds. It's crisp in my mind that an authentically compassionate and kind core is central, though I've also been a ball of negativity, vulgarity, and abuse. The discrepancy holds, yet I must refute some of what I think am.

I sometimes feel like a sad, sorry, and broken soul, I've played the poor me card all too often, and resilience and courage can replace that. Our lives cross the threshold to the pit, and I don't mean the religious hole. I instead suggest the sitting area in a home where some of our family and friends gather to create and celebrate in a few years.

My hope is Aeris meets Zeus, Belle, and Mooshka, and if adopted, I'll keep them each in my heart and being. Love isn't always enough to allow a positive relationship; we need to couple it with unity, respect and peace too.

I think I demonstrated love isn't enough with Natalie too. My overt attention and affection are like the years of saying "I love you" and calling out to remind Natalie she's beautiful and unique in my heart. How much of that love is real, though? I still don't know. I've doubted I'd even like her let alone want to live together with her for always.

Mom and Dad are right; I may need to care for myself first to do what's best. I know I can love things that are terrible for me, though Zeus moving in holds a fundamental premise of how to let things grow. I don't want to be enslaved or entrapped and, hopefully, I gather the freedom to do what we need to do to achieve our goals.

Remember to find people that want to work together *with* you in your life. As I refuse to make Zeus my entire focus, it may be a lesson of why I have so few in my life. I've been alone, not lonely, and I accept that it may be because I've not set myself aside so much. I wonder if it's best for me to be isolated yet don't think it is.

The music on the stereo was asking, "Do you think you're better off alone?" I'm not sure I can answer that. I've written about how living in a toxic relationship isn't better than living alone, and perhaps that's a sign left along the shoreline. We may be better off apart, and it's not fair about how I've been acting and behaving.

Is it because I don't talk enough? Is it because I refuse to make another the only focus of my life? I'm very much a solitary person, and I'm not clear about the pros and cons of having another living in my space. It's indeed something I've said I want, though how would I feel with so much connection and abundance of communication.

Winks and Boots were awesome and amazing cats. I adopted them in 2005 though they too were neglected by me. I get over-focused on my work, so maybe it's best I do live alone since I don't know how to love completely. Animals deserve love, kindness, and connection; different types than what I can sometimes give.

Humans are very different than cats, though do I find a female human to bond and connect with me? I hope she may talk and tell me her thoughts and feelings, and I hope we can have dialogues about how to build a future together. I'd love to have a partner to work with.

Intuition and clarity hone here. Understanding what is right can strengthen and shape the correct path, and a clear mind can more readily accept lessons and learn how to be patient and kind. I'd like to love in mutually beneficial ways, and I don't want to play just because I think I have to. Love and affection aren't great when another only wants their space and autonomy.

Even if I've not yet sensed in full the genuine love and magnificence of what life is, this work reminds me. We have a beautiful home, I do have my books, and faith cultivates our awareness. We learn about healthy boundaries and reciprocation; both positive and negative.

If we each sow the seeds of love, we can't expect them to sprout and harvest immediately. Sometimes we need to have patience, diligence, and determination. Gumption, devotion, and cultivated integrity atone with a place to sit and know other radical living beings. Home is a place for love. More people need love.

From the day Mom and I spoke, I heard tears in her voice. I needed an attitude adjustment and found my mental health has put us through so much. It doesn't feel right; Mom and I have been through massive fear, sadness, and concern through the years, though I continue to learn how to appreciate her for who she is instead of what I want to hear.

Mom, you've told me things to remember; such as to hold truth like a precious gem and to find ways to be happy. Thank you for allowing our life and thank you also for nudging me back to self-compassion instead of self-condemnation. Thank you for answering the phone and forgiving my self-obsessive and neurotic nature.

On Mother's day 2017, a person named Roy gave a valuable reminder. On that day, my heart turned towards my Mom in more honourable love. Roy reminded me that mothers are so vitally important and that they literally gave us life. Our Moms held us in their stomachs for months, and then we emerged into Earth. The reminder matters because it starts with real love, and I want to support that too.

With the premise of giving, we know it's a weird call of my being. Instead of telling me it's a stupid idea, instead, encourage me to follow my heart and give if I think it's right to do so. Crucial advice quoted at the close of the 8th Fountain: "The right thing, at the right time, for the right reason." In line with representation, also be guided to do the right things for the right people.

Although this is the 3rd three-part Fountain book, so much hasn't yet been seen or read by people. Barely anyone had read the books up to when I typed this, though honestly, how many

Fountain books are out there now? Dad may not like the idea of me buying books to share or sell, though I've kept the receipts of the books brought into Chilliwack.

About a thousand dollars of text is out there in the world, and I love when we coincide with good feelings. It's a trippy mix of personal faith, awareness, and consciousness. There is religious faith, yet couple both faith in God, the Universe, others, and also yourself to strengthen a holistic hope of all things combined.

Some people pray to God and wonder why their prayers aren't answered, though I think I understand how some say that 'the time isn't right.' In Gabby Bernstein's book, *The Universe Has Your Back* Gabby reminds us not to hound our prayers for completion; seeds need time to grow. Christy Whitman also reminds us to detach from expected outcomes as it's on God and the Universe's time, not ours, that we find our results.

In a more strict sense of time, we know that we may never really want it to be another's time to go. A lack of faith can't cover my projected fears or concerns over another person's situation, and I know how I get fearful. I understand some misgivings come from the point of love, though worries best not paint upon the walls of fate. We can shift destiny back to the wish we have many years of which to create.

By the time I finish writing this book, we hadn't yet met the results of how we evolve. Zeus was getting kinder and giving me more time to work on my books, and we continue to learn and adapt. My attitude adjustment about living with another needed hope and creative insight to be glad to be alive.

When the Sanctified Spirit version of *The Sands of Yesterday* completed in 2018, I felt a lot of negative feelings after finishing the book. It seemed like there was no work to perform and no purpose for living. Devotion and function can be fuel, and if I derive meaning from creating and providing shouldn't the consideration be to push onwards?

Strangely my core purpose benefits life in ways other than monetary support. I feel fulfilled knowing we each hold an essential meaning in life and dreamy, and wishfully, Italy calls me. I wonder about living overseas, though with whom shall I travel? Is this the home in which I'll always live? Some relationships, intuition, and guidance tell me the majority of my life hasn't even happened yet.

Differently, think of your primary friends from when you were a teen. Have you stayed in contact with them and cultivated friendships that also endure? Are you inspired to develop and tend new relationships that you have and shall have? Mom reminds me I do know a few people and that people are essential to me and how we live.

I've played the poor me card too much, though. I'm thankful Mom, Dad, and others put up with me, my neurosis and insecurities, and as parents and son, mine raised a good kid. I don't know if I'll ever fully 'adult.' I'm profoundly thankful for the patience and grace I receive, though I cover my heart knowing we must teach and allow others the same.

Mom, I love you, I am grateful for you, and I hope that what I put on the vision board manifests. I don't want you to be sad, and even if I disrespected you by disrespecting myself, I regather and reset. Others are not responsible for my feelings and thoughts; I am. How I choose to respond to my life is to love, share, and enjoy, and it *is* our opportunity to decide how we behave.

So as is, please forgive me. Forgive me for making life so much all about me and my issues, forgive me for the fears, tears, and years set apart from my heart, and as we heal and learn how to love better, I remember I can change and choose how to act and behave.

We find more ways to live, love, and give and develop a more accurate representation of how to be grateful for life. I wish you may thrive, and I send you some love too.

RECIPROCATION

There was an idea to write a chapter about resentments, yet resentment isn't a PLU8R word. It's best not to reciprocate resentments, even if we hold them, and I remind us we can feel resentful if we sacrifice too much of ourselves. With positive reciprocation, though, we may find an exchange for mutual benefit.

Sacrificing ourselves or seeking a compromise isn't reciprocation. We must find win/wins and give when we are thankful and because we want to. If we offer from a feeling or sense of obligation, we can feel resentful, so don't be a slave or prisoner to someone who gives expecting a return.

I know I can be a person to seek gain. I'm a self-absorbed person sometimes, though it's best I don't accuse others of such too. I also can be self-reflective and atone for my mistakes, yet that's linked to repentance and for a different chapter.

I told my Dad how I don't like how there's not more I can do for him. My Dad and I have a trippy relationship with the amount he's done for me than I have done for him too. Is that a parent thing? I want to learn how to love unconditionally with a selfless attitude so I can be a good parent also.

Resentment is a deep poison to drink. Irritation can damage ourselves or others with negativity, though I wonder where we may pour out grievances if we have them. One idea I've heard and recommended is to handwrite a letter with resentments and dislikes and then set the paper on fire. Releasing our negative thoughts and energies can help keep the waters of our being clean.

If we need to release and are confined with another when we want to be alone, we can't always ask the other to leave and come back home in a few hours. Some of our home mates have a right to be there too, and it's helpful to talk about our issues. I believe conversations help improve our quality of life, and I know it's not always possible.

For some, talking assists us by letting the other know exactly what we think and expect, and it benefits us too by receiving answers when we have questions. Some guesses could be correct, though to understand the full and entire truth of those we live with can aid us in working towards a positive resolution. Should the word resolution be a PLU8R word too?

Reciprocation also makes me think about global grace; what has been given or created that allows harmony between nations? Religion is something that crosses borders, though also can segment communities and human connection when beliefs differ.

My Dad's not a religious person, though he understands much about Earth and the political influences. My Dad lives overseas, so technology is a helpful way for us to keep in contact and bridge people between geographic locations. Though distortion can play a factor, my Dad doesn't believe in telepathy, even if it still seems like we're linked. I remember and remind us that my Dad is my Earthly father and not an omniscient deity.

I like how some watch the news and keep up to date and current with world events. I'm more microcosmic with irrational dreams, and if you've read the first few books, you've read about how I want to provide for many people. I know I've not done so yet. A weird twist about the significance and microcosm of this work, though, includes Zeus. Even though Zeus is just my cat, his relevance and importance are influential in how he affects this process.

Some beliefs may misdirect and mislead, and I think there are levels of contempt held over me from some in the local community. I wonder what to do to help improve the situation, and that's partly from where my charitable ideas sourced.

It may be a manipulation tactic, yet the thought is if we can provide for people, the interchange would allow us to live more freely. If I'm allowed to live the life I have, then my desire is others also receive grace and fantastic support too.

I'm grateful to have a home, food, water, income, and my creative work, and I'm also glad and thankful for my family, my friends, and my dreams. Home is a place to gather and create, and it's also a training ground for character qualities to grow and allow thoughts to manifest.

I may need more personal work to purge and cleanse some of my thoughts and feelings, though. I wish to provide clean and good energy and results, and since I've often been tainted and abused in the past, it's also a course in positive reciprocation and not retaliation.

A reactive nature isn't always kind. I've been goaded and triggered sometimes to the points of the outburst, and with some of the things that have happened to me and others, I wonder why God would ever allow those things to occur. I feel reluctant to worship someone who's allowed so much abuse.

Perhaps others haven't worshiped God because of their resentments about Him and what He's allowed? There have been atrocious actions and activities I don't condone, and it's hard to love someone who's allowed them to be. We may recognize concessions, repentance, and reparations for things we've done, yet an occasionally challenging nature may also wish reciprocation for transgressions.

Anger and outbursts can draw a particular judgement on ourselves, yet we can, sometimes, forgive. Some may not wish to allow grace; some may want to retaliate and take revenge, which also is not an R-word in PLU8R. Reverence is a PLU8R word, yet is best sourced from adoration, love, and respect for another, and not coerced by fear, abuse, or power.

What do you know about the positive and negative conspiracies? Am I being used as a puppet and pawn for a purpose beyond my comprehension? Why have I come so close to death to be again granted an extension of life here on Earth? If positive reciprocation and reciprocity are reasons I'm alive, I'd like to make reparations and show my gratitude for being allowed to live.

Up to writing this, I haven't provided so much for others. I commit to regather, rejuvenate and recover when I can, though how shall this evolve at home? Do I get past my self-defeating behaviour and language and excel? Is the bookwork a waste of time, or are these books seeds that sprout, flourish, and grow? Is this positively persistent and bullish, or is this bullshit, and we should subsist?

Obsessions can twist actions and produce compassion and empathy, yet if we forgive and forget our fates, do we still get sick and tired of proclamations and assumption? Can we please call of a tiny point of hope to allow me to keep writing?

In August 2018, I didn't have many mutually loving relationships. A sharp inkling tells me it was a mistake to even think of giving up on my cat. A defiant nature says: "forget it, keep the cat and thrive" while the doubt says, "how will you ever thrive Rob?" Thoughts and insecurities must be from a source different than my DNA.

The name of my cat compounds this. How can so much dramatic significance and neurotic, obsessive nature fuel from the point of just one entity's name? "Hey, Zeus" is not the Spanish Jesus. By discussing the idea, the premise amplifies and compounds, yet a sway from belief finds it's worth going through discomfort and learning.

By writing to you, we see messages from others weave into the relationships we have. Does Zeus think of me as a Dad to him? The statement "I wish you were here, Dad" makes me feel sad as some have already lost their fathers. By being out of the home, are the potential and future moments of happiness worth the uncomfortable feelings and thoughts?

As Zeus does stay here, we form and maintain a life we love and are thankful to have. With previous cats Winks and Boots, they contracted leukemia. I thought it was because they didn't want to live here anymore and because they were alone so often. Was that the reason they got sick; or is disease a legitimate thing?

My concerns compel me to either sacrifice everything to cater to some or opt out to deny myself the responsibility for another's life. Even as this formed, mixed attitudes, energies, and beliefs were working with faith; this is a spatial and unique present.

Do we understand and accept others shall focus? Do people feel sad and neglected? If I'm so blatantly dismissive of my responsibilities, such as parenting a cat, how could I ever expect a woman to agree to live with me? If I focus on my books and keep myself apart, how can I be part of our communities? Would it be different if we could speak?

I don't know how some accept me for who I am, and I also wonder if it's because Dad's so far away that he doesn't see how I am here on Earth. We're an ocean apart, and I parallel that with others. There's the ocean of work separating us, yet are the rare contact points between us worth as much as they can be? Yes.

Concerns for sanity and emotional wellbeing seeped into this Fountain. If my Dad is the pinnacle and influential person as he is to me up to now, and we keep a positive reciprocal relationship, can we show powerful words and work may become more than ourselves? Yes.

What though if people turn against us or get angry? That wouldn't be good. My waffling and wavering tips a mind forward, in and away from what the reality *is*, not what it shall be. From the chapter *Buckle Up Koyich* in the 6th Fountain: *There is the explicit freedom that can be lost or gained by making or changing commitments.* I don't know what the correct choices are and have been wrong countless times.

What even is the point of writing these books? They seem to be a linear path of objectives to meet, yet I haven't blazed those trails. Are we on the wrong bus or train? Should we be on a different pathway? Do I realize what the potential of these works is? The potential, yes, though should I sacrifice all of what *I* want and instead focus entirely on other people's wants and provide? Perhaps.

What do these brief flashes of déjà vu mean? Do they say we're on the correct and finite path? Are they telling us we need to learn the lesson again? Are they just prophetic fragments of time stemmed from full-fledged neurotic obsession? As we weave my insecurities into the pages of text, we find clarity and cleansing, and if we can comprehend different viewpoints and pass our fears, we can see the truth. I then must share it with the world.

Can I know, please, whether I am doing the right things for the right reasons? Even if there's doubt and I'm way out of proper timing, is this work playing in the mud, or helping purify the water to present life for many on Earth?

A clear statement about reciprocation again; we exchange value mutually to benefit each other. I seem a bit challenged about the offer, yet remember choices are for individuals to make. We cannot force others to work with us, similar to how we cannot force a seed to grow.

It's also explicitly clear that when we're pissed off, it's far less likely we'll play. We'll check in about how the situation unfolds, yet by the time I finish this, much shall have occurred. Perhaps by the time this book releases we'll have reached the next level of giving for Providing Point; $50 a month pledges.

Some people said to adopt Zeus out again, yet the carrot of a prosperous and happy future lured me into keeping him. Was it a wise choice, or me being greedy? I need someone to love, though is the conceived viewpoint accurate? Am I capable of love, or are the projected beliefs not understanding what the truth is? It's difficult to know.

This Fountain is the third in the Fountains of Fortitude. Part of my belief thought I needed to let my cat go so fortify a positive future. Some, and not just my cat, remind me if we affect one life abundantly well, that that's more worthwhile than having a million followers. What if we do both?

Most of us don't like being controlled by others, and some can be controlling. It's obvious we can't manage some and tell them what to do, so is it best to shift along the shoreline and focus on what we can do no matter who it's for? If I don't want to feel spite or hatred, is it best to release?

I have been angry, though keep from that emotion as I learn how to deal with self-control and avoid being controlled. I recall past misbehaviours and refrain from becoming cold, cynical, and distant. A thought on the patio had me say, "I've made you too important in my life." It's a very factual statement of Natalie too. I don't think either Zeus or Natalie thoroughly knows or appreciates how I've cared for them both, even if I've had an idea to shed them.

Dad told me to give up on Natalie many years ago, and Zeus has been a vital point by being in my life. How could I give up on having a real live entity in my home? I'm glad I kept Zeus, though a fact also is I've never heard either Zeus or Natalie speak an entire sentence to me.

Natalie felt like real love when her spirit and mine melded, though I think she wishes to be free of my thoughts and me. My tainted views from decades ago taunt me with the urgency of devotion that I can't show to some I know. A few have loved me unconditionally, and for doing so, they also shall receive my full regard with additional reciprocation.

RECIPROCITY

I'm thankful the truth arrives. I didn't think I could receive real love from the two names mentioned in the previous chapter, so I rationally removed my attachments to one of them and live with the other.

When I told Zeus I wasn't going to play any more one night, he started a kitty tantrum. He'd been clawing the furniture and ripped around the apartment frantically. I think the other name was upset at me too, though for the right reasons. If others are spiteful, it's best I don't reciprocate, and perhaps it's best to give them the freedom to express.

Part of me believes that some have wanted me dead, though I've thought it's because they want to be free of my thoughts. One thing about the spiritual realm is that I don't know if my mind could haunt others if I'm gone. I don't know what life is like in the afterlife.

It seems I've disturbed people in the living world, and perhaps living and honing my focus and work disrupts some. I've thought my books could be imperative, though the market indeed hasn't said that yet. Foolish intuition and delusions assure me my work is for the good of this planet even if the results up to now say otherwise.

This chapter was titled Rationalization, though I changed it to Reciprocity. When I looked up the word rationalization, it showed that rationalization is not what I want to do; rationalization is self-justification and making excuses. Invented excuses have had me justifying years of attachment to someone I've never had a conversation with, yet. Must I explain why I haven't done what's needed to have a real connection?

I've abused grace and blessings, and I almost want to turn this chapter into secular repentance. Is it an idea to shift to religion again? If I directed the first pages to a specific person, must I force this work to be okay? Rationalization tells me some have admired my perseverance and that the world needs people like me. Is that honestly true, or am I trying to make myself feel good?

We can help guide people to feel or think positively about themselves, though I'm also crisply aware that one point of damage can ruin everything. I've been abrash sometimes too often, and I fear I'm not gentle enough to not crumble a psyche. My visible deflection of character staunches repentance about some vitally valid faults.

My errors, mistakes, and offensive thoughts call for me to keep away from engaging with some in mainstream society. Am I to be accepted? Am I to be fringe? How can success be gleaned if I don't put myself out there into the world?

Maybe that's part of the rationalization; that I should be kept away from society and denied love and luck. If I can't have and give authentic and genuine peace, love, unity, or respect, then is that why I've believed best be alone writing in a vacuum. When shall clarity hone and have me get past myself and help other people like you?

A friend brought me to her church the most recent Saturday before writing this. I'm thankful for her doing so as my spiritual faith, prayer, and practice had been lacking in the previous weeks. Bringing me to a church and partaking in communion reminded me of God and how I revere and need to repent; I don't want to rationalize.

I want to make amends and haven't spoken to God so much recently. I've had fragmented awareness and action, and haven't been praying very often. *Should I shift from you and write the rest of this chapter to God?*

Lord, thank You. I'm sorry for not trusting in You, I'm sorry for not resting and resetting myself, my heart, and my mind and for seeking my benefit, and I'm sorry for not setting myself aside and working for the greater good. And for the lives of this planet, I'm sorry for not always asking for guidance.

Thank You for Your sacrifice and for reminding me Earth is home for more than just my cat, my friends, my family, and me. I'm sorry for not putting myself and my needs aside and for wanting Zeus to adapt to me. I also repent for not putting in the work needed to thrive.

I'm still a dramatically flawed human, and although tears rarely pass across my countenance, I thank You for reminding me of my mistakes and my remorse. Naturally, we allow beauty and brilliance to manifest, though if the process forces my convictions, I open my being to forgiveness. I haven't trusted You and how You care for me too. Grazie sempre, Dio. Amen.

Instinct can deflect and hide the truth sometimes. We may not always be happy with who we are, and I know I've had terrible thoughts and ideas in my awareness. I've not submitted to the will of Heaven; to allow myself to be a channel and conduit for what God wishes and wants to happen on Earth.

I've rarely sought to know God's desires, and I've been wayward and filled with disdain. In the times when we meet negativity and brashness, please let there be self-control. Evil is a thing of Earth too, yet never let us have it within ourselves or in our hearts. Let us learn how to be pure, clean water and light to nurture and nourish.

(Insert 90 ½ hours between points of formation)

The chemicals call. Cigarettes and coffee draw me as time is a mixture of their energy. I feel them urge me to stay up and create, yet when the addictive nature of writing, caffeine, and cigarettes adjusts the course of time, weird things happen.

Most of the Fountain books have formed during late nights, and even if I'm not smoking inside my apartment, the tar bars crawl on the patio nudging me to create. A challenging nature lures me to pull in the toxic substances.

The days often find me up and out of bed late with a few calls from the snooze button. The lessons and activities from being up and at 'er and performing a full work day found a few blessings; the first Amazon copies of *The Sands of Yesterday* and *Etched in Stone* sold one day I put in the work.

Rationalizations swerve me from pushing myself back on the tracks of 7:30 AM wake up times and going to bed at 10 PM. Is staying up late a way to lay future pathways? I seem to think so, though I don't know how the results can shift until later in the process of discovering.

Self-awareness can be for mutual gain, and it may be I'm again seeking my benefit as I find myself swaying between activities. From what is right and propper, I swing between different sides of behaviour as we balance between the moments of the past, present, and future.

At the SnowPeaks Toastmasters group, Josie asked me if I accept my past and what I think about it. My answer showed dejection. My history is tainted, and because I don't like some of my past, a conversation with another friend reminded me of something else — the friend's reminder combined with what Jay Sethi said on episode 608 of Lewis Howes' podcast *The School of Greatness*.

Jay says to remember the good things people have done for us and remember the bad we have done to others. Jay also suggests we not be overconfident.

A writing lesson here:
1) Write often.
2) Write what you mean.
3) Trust is risky.
4) We can learn to accept ourselves if we tell our truth.

I'm sometimes afraid of my truths, though I'd like to learn more through safe fear. Safe fear may be an alternate term for vulnerability and is a concept to explore. When we admit our faults to another or reveal our past, even to ourselves, we can feel insecurities — acceptance is helpful.

If I reveal my truths and I don't like the facts, I can fear an adverse judgement, though if I'm too busy or neglect to process such, I may try to ignore or justify. That rationalization could be like sweeping the dirt under the rug, and when we need to treat and resolve faults or fractures, ignoring the issues may not be beneficial.

In the closing chapter of the 5th Fountain, I mention seven words from PD Seminars; Breathe, Aware, Acknowledge, Accept, Action, Appreciate, and Humour. As I become aware, acknowledge, and accept, I then can choose how I'll resolve issues and clean up my act. Hopefully, later we can appreciate the changes and have a good laugh or two.

I want to type more about learning our truth by uncovering answers. Adjustment and acceptance may find some people don't admit mistakes, yet with trust, even if risky, we may help ourselves and others heal. One chapter in this book is called Repentance, yet we're not there yet. I've repented in other books; it's part of how I admit and reveal. From Jay Sethi's advice to remember our wrongs and an Alcoholics Anonomys step, that may be what the Repentance chapter is.

Some dreams I've had and things I've written about can be considered entirely foolish. Lewis spoke in one episode about how some have faith in God while others have confidence in themselves. Is that my impulse? It's a contrast that my bald human audacity presumes I can make a change while God uses me; cultivating imposed restrictions to expand my capacity.

Is it because a person of faith believes cosmic powers have an intended purpose for us? Is addressing problems still a way to weave around accepting them? Do some people feel complete tranquillity and peace after they allow fate to unravel, and then have nothing to say?

"Frozen in the keys is a breeze of mp3s from the Underground Sea's."

My rhymes are part of me and who I am, though some may not like them. If others don't want to hear the words, can they still be accepted? A question of us each too, if we don't love ourselves, can we not learn to at least understand ourselves? I hope that we each learn to accept ourselves; even the parts we don't like. Hopefully, we can choose how to act more appropriately.

It's weird too because there are many things I've liked that I've not accepted; love, money, and generosity. My overly self-focused nature occasionally obsesses and has had an aversion to receiving things. Fear of being accepted can cause reclusive behaviours by not putting myself out there.

Rationalization, repentance, or revelation? Am I held away from telling the truth because there are facts of love in our youth? Written somewhere is a different idea; to keep secrets away from some to surprise them with wondrous goodness in the future. If things start fantastic and at their best, there sometimes can only be room for deterioration.

To metaphors, what of sine waves and how they graph? Starting at zero, the point of our inception, we then climb upwards into happiness (positive). The timeline then levels out and cross back down to be zero and then deep into the depths of despair (negative). Things again balance out, and we surface again from a neutral state lifting into positivity for the next cycle.

Electricity is linked to negativity, though if we use positive power, can we find useful and helpful functions? Do I remain an electron coursing through live wires to conduct the energy of truth, or do I develop as a proton to be part of a core nucleus? Must I be transient, or can I be more stable and secure in a more central location?

Dreams surged back. The Survivor dream was luring me again. Though I don't want to be on TV, a precious part of me wants to compete on the show to experience the forging of character. A U.S. citizen only rule was in action when their casting agent asked me for a written application on September 11th, 2017, for the second layer of screening. They denied me because of my citizenship, though they accept Canadian contestants now.

One reason I apply to Survivor is that if they permit me to compete, I've promised to quit smoking. It's highly unlikely I contend, yet encouragement to experience the dream, no matter how unrealistic, also impels me. I admit I see the game as an external motivation to become smoke-free.

I was compiling my most recent Survivor application video when I first wrote the base of this chapter. I uploaded the video to put another seed out to the winds of Earth; specifically the casting department of CBS.

"Make a wish they said.
Let it grow, they say.
If we don't ask for what we want,
Miracles may be taken away."

I wonder how and if that seed shall sprout and grow. The request I have is that it may.

ROBERT KOYICH

RECOGNITION

Recognize words are tools constructed by forces of instinct. Between each letter, behaviours are tracked and mapped with cognition. There also are omissions of how we use them.

Precarious tendencies of fate lure future events, yet *Fragments of Intent* holds well. We endure, persevere, and complete our work developing from *The Sands of Yesterday*.

Chilliwack seems to have a split between friends. Some don't contact, few do, and some are angry that I've been living freely. Some also are rare gems that support me and are allured by what I create. We know these books don't form on their own, though. They are a consecrated production linked to many.

There's a curiosity about some of these thoughts and activities. Up to May 2019, few have processed what I've keyed, yet the printed forms hold a symbiotic creation and formation sometimes. There are inceptive edits and moments of selection while the community and consect don't always seem to meld in PLU8R.

Peace holds like a static trapeze, and while some of the working population is angry with me, there also are some who are unemployed that are equally agitated. Why should I have luxuries when others can't afford to eat without having to work full-time? Disparity oscillates in mind.

I don't believe I'm *entitled* to the life I have, though am grateful to thrive. I'm exceptionally fortunate and lucky to have what I have, and concern spins some woven threads in this Introversial loom. Authorship *is* a profession and vocation, yet it's not earned me an income up to this release. I've also not worked at it full-time.

I'm an example of grace, yet I too am not fond of how far I've come without earning my pay. It's a great belief I am on a path of profitable authorship, yet I need to find an alternate source of income because books haven't yet sold.

There's a question: why write more books if sales haven't occurred? If the majority of the earnings go to charity, what is my motivation? If I continue with authorship as a profession and vocation and not random interest, wouldn't it be better to write knowledge-based books or compelling fiction to entertain?

Marketing for soliciting sales or pledges aren't my passionate desire, and I admit I've not asked many people to contribute. I'd like and love to sell books and had pushed a bit on Facebook, yet I feel grimy to ask. I've driven away friends and contacts by asking them to be patrons or book purchasers, and even if intents are there, things haven't lined up correctly.

When these books form, they seem like the right things too. If being part of the community, succeeding in finding an audience, and also having regular employment is a good plan, I must hold firm to the idea. I can work part-time, take a course at University, and also continue to form these books with a release of attachment to earning only for others.

Providing Point is an excellent program, yet not what I want to focus on full-time. The program can do some good in the local community, so I keep the program open, and I also keep the program open because most of the Fountains books have links for people to contribute. I'm okay to perform the required tasks to keep Providing Point open, I'm not, though, compelled or committed to fundraising.

Recognizing and accepting reality may be a key to happiness. If we can gather the parameters for shared prosperity, it's primary to care for the love and wellbeing of our friends, family, and communities as well as ourselves. There's the saying 'love don't cost a thing' which reminds us we can give in ways other than money. It tips me into recalling we can reach out to people without intents to solicit gain. We can give just by being a friend.

Because I've messaged or called so few, is that why so few have also called out to me? I recognize the peaceful and careful sides of self; there's peace while understanding anger flares from time to time too. It's best not to possess any resentments or emotions that can lead to hate, so I prefer to keep away from some people and situations. I need to restrict contact with some while remembering others.

I distil and hope to refine my nature and purify my thoughts and how I've been. Although Earth doesn't seem to want me here at times, it may be because the loving and peaceful ones are guarding and keeping secrets from the mind. Sometimes fear winds into nervousness, and hate and despair are legitimate concerns. Even if I don't wish bad things for others, I know some may be mad at me for my behaviours.

Subconscious effects can reflect the past and negative self-worth. Karma from distant years may call retribution, yet retribution isn't part of PLU8R ethics. PLU8R is a concept that meshes this together, and though most don't know the term, we pass along the string of infinity reminding this is where we are.

Through the past weeks, I'd not been entirely okay with my life and situation. Releasing attachments is helpful, and a lucidly carried idea accepting that my work may not be understood or appreciated yet. The construction of these books share values I insist on contributing though.

Recently, I've heard a few different friends' voices in my mind, plus a few online mentors. These internal voices cued me to ask a kind and cool friend if they'd ever heard my voice in their mind. What they told me I'm a warning sign for them to be more aware.

I wrote a chapter called *Community and Consect* in the 5th Fountain to a cousin who used to hear my voice in her mind. When she was growing up; she told me I was her conscience. My voice would say 'don't do that' in her thoughts even though I had zero conscious awareness of her and what she was doing back then.

It makes me wonder, what are the facts about inner voices and telepathy? Are we all delusional schizophrenics believing in sounds, tones, and the thoughts of others? Are our thoughts who we are, or am I projecting delusions of grandeur and being paranoid about safe things and people? Even religious people claim they must decipher what God or the enemy is in their thoughts. I barely ever hear the voice of God in my mind.

I've thought others also hear voices and I believe schizophrenic people might be people who didn't learn about telepathy when they were younger. I've thought I was lied to about its existence, and my psychosis Christmas 2017 was extreme. I went crazy and called beliefs about mass conspiracy as thoughts held a projected idea that the life of Earth itself was in jeopardy.

I've had legitimate concerns including deluded thinking, mental hallucination, and religious mislabelling. The thoughts carrying on in mind are not all our own, yet we also may be tripping on false assumptions. Judgmental accusations and twisted understanding have had people believing falsities and basing wrong actions on those beliefs.

I think we all should encourage and have compassion, understanding, and love. I believe we all can practice sharing grace and forgiveness more often too. I also guess some cannot convey their goodness and honest truths because of corruption. If we can clean the wreckage of our past and heal trauma, we also must be cautious of soliciting judgment based only on thought.

Generational trauma is legitimate. People fuse with the damage and dramas of generational links, and it reminds us Earth has a filthy past in some ways. From one generation to the next, DNA theoretically holds some of the corrupted data and attitudes, yet I believe we may heal ourselves and our views.

Choose to heal and purify your mind, being, soul, spirit, and heart. If we can work for a combined improvement and protection of life, I'd like and love for all people to be authentically kind and decent. On Earth, there is a multitude of some who aren't, yet we can choose how we live and respond. Collective improvement in life is possible.

Mom used to criticize, condemn, and complain, yet she's healed and changed. Mom's always loved me; she just used to project her fears and concerns onto me. I used to cause her all sorts of trauma and angst, yet I evolved, and now Mom's accepting, encouraging, kind, and compassionate to me.

I appreciate and like how my Mom has changed through the years, yet honestly, I don't know about all the woes and sadness she secretly carries in her heart. Not so strangely, Dad has been consistent over the past decades. He hasn't always believed I could succeed with music or books, though he's still open to helping and supporting me.

My Dad keeps bright, optimistic, and cheery even when some things are not all well. Dad's also commented about admiring my persistence with these books. He brings me to visit him every one or two years and keeps in phone and message contact, and though Dad can have a critical nature of my appearance and lifestyle, similar to my Mom has been with fear, I know he does it from the point of love.

This Fountain started on the topic of my cat, Zeus, and I know I've not yet earned his love. We've adjusted mainly well and are okay, though I'm still sometimes over-focused and not always open or actively engaged with him. I appreciate Zeus' company and hope he's okay with me.

From how I've been a cat-parent, I recognize how I may not be a great human parent. I can't imagine yet what it's like to set aside my entire life for another to actively engage, support, and raise them. I don't know if I ever find a gal and also have a kid with her.

Subtle symbiotic references linger. Have you heard the theory every living being and thing is an extension of our subconscious mind? Every sight or sound can be thread weaving our consciousness. I'd love to hear Zeus speak English and answer my questions because I'd like to know his truths. He also could tell me what he wants.

I pray to God, yet I barely ever hear his voice, yet that may be because I'm still over-focused on my thoughts and I'm afraid to hear. In the past, I've thought God's quite angry at me, and with some of the things I've felt and experienced, it makes me question why he'd allow such things to happen to a person he's said to love.

It's only recently I've been thinking of Heaven and Hell more often. Even if I'd prefer to stay on Earth, I believe that both realms are active and pulling chords of life on Earth. Some people theorize that Earth life is just a purgatory or afterlife from our previous existence, yet current life seems genuinely real.

In the psych ward, I thought I was in an afterlife, and earlier in the day when I wrote this, I wondered if I was going onto the next life. I've had nights where I thought I was transferring to Heaven, and I'm afraid to leave my current existence. I don't know if releasing me would mean it would all end, or if there are still decades of action and activity for me to live here on Earth.

When I've been writing or working on books, I've felt a lack of purpose. At other times when I open up the computer to type or edit, I believe it's the right and correct thing to do with my energy; to create. I want to be more consistent with my beliefs and with myself too.

I appreciate the stability of knowing what to do and planning my days before they arrive could be a habit to regain. I want to become more reliable, yet others may need me to engage by being up and active. My apathy is an excuse for being sporadic sometimes, though I've often woken up in the morning with zero ideas as to what I'll do or what I want to happen.

Some people think they'd love to have no job and have fully open days, yet an abundance of time has found me uncertain and directionless at times. The online mentors assure us to work and hustle, and when I get to the plow, and into the pages, I feel inspired to write and edit. If I don't have a person to talk with to plan, talk, process, or build, though, I've found it a bit hopeless and empty.

Working on the books is something, though if profits are the metric to gauge their worth, results haven't yet shown they're valuable. An exact and precise theory and explanation for a shared Freedom Solution isn't relevant if no one else reads, supports, or allies to activate it.

A Gary Vaynerchuk idea is that people are the ROI. If we don't use or manipulate life or people purely for our gain, we can return to ethical marketing and reciprocation. If part of the purpose is to provide for people, not just time and resources, we must find what we can give.

It's great that we can find some mutual benefits by using these books as a conduit. My Dad's advice from January 2018 includes earning and caring for myself first before I can give and assist others. I seem to think we can do both.

Even if my books aren't yet recognized as productive for being a member of society, I endure with a verbose layer of text reminding the sound's keys are a pathway to peace and prosperity.

RELEVATION

Re*lev*ation is an invented language word. Its original meaning was to enjoy something thoroughly; to revel in it. Re*vel*ation is a different word, and doesn't use the term revel as its base; or does it?

We enjoy our pleasures, as I soak up the coffee or tea and cigarettes. I think of how vices can be crucial for our wellbeing and derived enjoyment, and though we glean truth from what we enjoy, we may need to rethink what we do. As it stands, relevation is an R-word of PLU8R.

Realization could be a PLU8R word, though not in the definition of realizing by being aware of thing; that's more in line with recognition. Instead, when we recognize and activate our dreams and ambitions into reality, we can see and experience some fantastic stuff.

Truth is a beautiful and fickle thing, though. In the past few days, I've realized some things in the awareness definition of realization. Some are aware of how I've been living and are potentially angry with me for living the life I live. I can't say it's a life I'm leading, because few are following at this point and I've not been a great role model.

When my previous social work professor Darrell and I spoke, he agreed with some of my views. The cliché term of 'it's the journey, not the destination' rings in with the idea that we should enjoy life. It echoes in my soul that people are not happy, and my fear may be a neurotic response to projected ideas that stem from jealousy. There's a need to act and behave ethically, and if we do, we may not have judgments and opinions cross us into a feared quandary.

Regarding my work situation and PWD designation, I'd need to earn more than $1,000 a month more before my governmentally provided income would reduce. My goal of being self-sufficient affirms my ambition to make $3,000 a month on my own so that I can make my way and not rely on others to support.

The dramatic concerns and fears I carry of the plan and the plot may be where my paranoia's tweak. If I'm receiving financial assistance and workers are angry at me for such, I'll need to find a pathway different than writing to earn. According to current results, books are not the path.

Mathematically I need to sell about a thousand books per month to earn $3,000 a month, and yet with the urgency of a daunted camel, I'm not clear where I can draw water to provide for myself. What about those others I've wished to nourish?

I think my charitable plans are moot up to this point and have called others to be upset at me for failing with the programs because I've not provided shelter for people yet. Reverting to the R-word rationalization, I don't know if ignoring the sounds and voices seemingly aimed at me is ignorance or sound thinking. I've reached a point that if I sense any negativity aimed at me, I think it's from sources of my corrupted data.

If our conscience guides us, perhaps it's a reflexive fear that shows I've not always attuned to love and positive reciprocation. Instead, I've sometimes thought that retribution is what my karma holds. Perhaps there's silence from the just, confident, and loving people from their concerns, yet with the result of isolation and separateness, I wonder how I can again choose to love.

Gary chips into my mind again with the idea, wish, and recommendation to 'make positivity louder.' Conversely, it may be right that some keep silent to assure peace is maintained. The tendency to believe some dislike any form of sound guides me to shine out some quiet light and goodness.

Maybe it is a big dangerous world, and a marshmallow like me is afraid of getting tossed in the fire. The crispy outside of a burnt soul may show blackened remains of what once was a kind and genuine treat. We may not be able to un-char a burnt marshmallow, yet if we shed the outer layer, it still can be a kind treat if adequately handled.

We can't reverse time, yet there are reminders that we can choose how to act moving forward. If kindness, inclusion, and goodness are my values, and I've not seemed to hold those three qualities, perhaps there is some cognitive or karmic distortion. If I accept 100% responsibility for my life, how shall I behave differently?

Many people blame others for the situations in their lives, and some even denounce or feel negative when good fortune happens for another. I'm not entitled to the beautiful things I have and experience, yet I also wish not to be condemned, chastised, or corrupted by those who haven't been so fortunate either.

Acceptance is a substantial value, yet seemingly not so widely practiced, even by myself. I've been judgmental of others and how they live their lives, yet I don't often intercede and sometimes avoid making direct accusations. Maybe that's what's happening to me? People may accept my choices, yet not like them and carry their animosity desiring to keep away.

We mustn't presume that everything we sense is purely about us, though. Crossfire and shrapnel from other people's battles sometimes can taint and damage us. We can't be entirely responsible for other people's choices, yet we each have a decision and influence on how we'll act and respond to them.

Self-responsibility and self-acceptance meld into personal ethics with self-awareness. By knowing what we like, and what we need to do, then acting accordingly with our morals and plans, we can and shall build well. I hadn't yet written the repentance chapter in this book, though need to bring the lens back a bit from the canvas.

The brushstrokes over my life are not all painted by my hand. Some have splashed red paint across my mind, and now it's my responsibility to finger paint with the keys. I must remind us that part of what I draw is hearts and diamonds while some may seem to attract a club or spade.

If someone throws green at me, I can twist it towards casting with an Emerald, yet I think some of this burns truth into my awareness. I don't want to rely on chemicals or colour associations to understand, and I want to learn how to think like clean water again.

The premise of being a single node isn't one I often explain, yet it's shaped and moulded me to who I am. I'm not so cunning to plot or plan against others, yet I've also thought and acted like I'm separate and distinct from life when it's a vast integrated network. I don't often see or think of many that are part of life's fabric, and pokey claws remind me to stop stitching together the tapestry.

If we hold on and share the quilt, are the mental punctures of my consciousness an actual attack, or are they lurking judgments for other reasons? Are my impressions of a telepathic network allying for me in secrecy part of a real conspiracy? I've sometimes thought that many others wish to live and thrive freely to activate some of the principles I've presented.

My charitable work is the pinnacle of my purpose, though perhaps the incubation process is keeping me held in my time cell with my lovable feline friend. I can't prove theories alone, and I can't convince people about them either. Perhaps conspiring to provide is protection to assure I may have what I need too?

There may be a different R, relevance, which procures me to carry back to natural progression instead of pre-formulated ideas and premises. I'd been rehashing *Fragments of Intent* to rerelease the book in October 2018, and I did so. Revisiting the book seemed to hold me back. I need to seed new actions, text, and behaviours, yet my encrypted beliefs also help assure I follow through with my commitments.

Little inklings of hope had sprouted near the middle of September 2018. The first three copies of *The Sands of Yesterday* and two transcripts of *Etched in Stone* had sold online.

In the 6th Fountain's chapter *Buckle Up Koyich*, I told my audience that 100% of the earnings from individual Fountains go to different charities. They do. *Seeds of Tomorrow*'s profits go to Providing Point, *Fields of Formation*'s go to Pencils of

Promise, yet I'd not yet said what *A Distant Glimmer* and *Etched in Stone* fund.

The earnings from *A Distant Glimmer* go to the Dream Fund to provide dream items for people, and *Open to Fate* go to Ruth and Naomi's, a street-level mission to provide food and shelter. If I allow myself to get dreamy again, my fantasy and hope are many books sell. Business ideas remind me some entrepreneurs have multiple businesses covering different groups and services, and that's kind of how my books are; they are a diversified network of potential giving and providing.

If we are to sell many thousands of books and Patreon helps with Providing Point, then can we not support more people? In the months before this. I found I'd like to have Seed money for friends in need too and not just the street level. The $5 per person concept from the speech *The Seed* in the 8th Fountain is still a great idea, though not only the homeless or street population needs additional support.

I think of two friends who've needed bus passes or food and haven't been able to afford them on their own. My friend Chandra and I talked about *Etched in Stone* and how it could be used to finance people's wants other than the homeless. Creative luxury and, yes, wishful thinking have allocated the earnings from 7th Fountain, *Etched in Stone*, towards gifts to friends who need some support.

If I reveal some of my most outlandish imaginations, perhaps we can write them into life. That may be what the next three Fountains are; *The Fountains of Fantasy*. Some may accuse me of being whimsical up to now, though can we not expand our dreams? It's also weird I'm such a dreamer while being up at 1:45 AM working obsessively on these books.

One night when I was happy and enthused about my creative work and process, I imagined that if I could provide enough resources and support to others, that people who are in a far higher financial and influential position would supply me with a car. I fantasized that not only would books thrive and excel, though that I'd also receive rewards for my efforts.

If we go back to previous wishes, I want to earn enough

money that I can share 99% of what I make. As foolish as that may seem, it's appeared at brief moments in my thoughts as entirely logical and rational. I may get audacious, though I write to activate my ability to thrive.

Could the Fountains yet be the water that allows other seeds to thrive? Even if not in the gardens and fields I know, creating these books is quite an involved process. I sometimes enjoy making these books, and at other times I feel awash editing and revising wondering 'why am I even doing this?' Some moments of fresh hope, faith, and awareness cleave to my being too when I type, even if people don't need to know about my life.

Sometimes it seems like people are latched onto my thoughts and pillaging my consciousness. Code words and lyrics can fragment my thoughts, however, when deciphered, they don't always lead to feeling secure. Relevating in the sheer audacity the universe holds for me, I am grateful. I am thankful, blessed, and fortunate to have what I have, to do what I do, and to know what I know.

There may be some who dislike my freedom and styles of writing or living, yet there also are some who know the worth is not often understood or appreciated. Providing Point and the Fountains are purposed for other people, yet I hope to gather for myself too.

(Insert three weeks between tending)

Survivor accepts Canadians now? On February 5th, 2015, I gave a challenge to Jeff Probst via Twitter. As you read in the chapter Reciprocation, you may know what the deal is; if I'm accepted to compete, I quit smoking to be allowed to play. If permitted to struggle in the sand, I think to write a book to track the preparations and experiences of how I achieve full physical health again.

I've smoked for 25 years and seem to think I need a dramatic impetus to quit. Survivor is that, and I am terrified about it. I've heard that when we don't get nervousness or get butterflies, it shows we don't care, and in the previous eight weeks to this, I had lost a lot of vigour, vitality, and desire to live and thrive. I've felt worthless and functionless since professional authorship and my Seed work hasn't sprouted, so I reset, regather, and yes, I am a David.

If we expect nothing and want everything, we may be sadly disappointed. If we learn to be glad about anything and don't expect anything then miracles, surprises, and bonus points are our reward. If we can learn to be grateful, happy, and thankful with anything, we also shall appreciate what we receive knowing we are not entitled to such. Is this how to accept blessings? If we act and behave well to gain well, is that being manipulative with the cosmic energies of karma?

Zeus called me into my mind again. I set such a high set of standards and expectations for Zeus in the first weeks he was here. My current natural behaviour contrasts that now dramatically as I gave Zeus undivided attention and connection for almost the entire day for the early few days. Now, I've barely given much at all.

I want to be confident and kind and improve my behaviours. With my friends and contacts, I've learned and adapted to expect little from them, so anything I receive as attention from them is appreciated. Some dearly loved friends have treated me like I have Zeus, carrying on with their lives and not reaching out.

The ideal situation is to elevate and relevate; to lift people up and to thoroughly enjoy and appreciate our lives. As I learn to actively cherish and revel in our relationships and dreams as much as I have consumable pleasures, we can improve the qualities of our experience.

ROBERT KOYICH

210

REVELATION

I revel in my sanity while remembering others who want everyone to have a life they love, cherish, and adore. I'm a thankful person and gladdened when others have what they like and want, yet I also feel biased against myself for having more than others. I learn to get over that.

Even if I'm not jealous or envious of multimillion-dollar earners, I've feared others earning more than I do are jealous or envious of me. My income in 2017 was $22k, and I'm aware I have an abundance of time. I'm also mindful that some who have less money than I do have love and can care fiercely. I want to learn how to love and care more too.

In my creative writing course in Fall 2018, I found I'm not great at writing. On our first assignment, a non-fiction piece, I received a C grade on a paper about unresolved childhood issues. I thought I've been daft for considering profitable authorship is my path, though I've not always known what my way or purpose is.

My cat was blitzing around the apartment, angry because I was working on the computer. I neglect Zeus so much, and I know my self-derived actions and impulses are ruining myself with caffeine and nicotine. I seem to think I need drastic purpose and almost call myself into destruction with chemicals. Perhaps Restraint is an R-word to use in PLU8R? I've not yet realized how some of my desires have such dramatic costs.

These books stemmed from a gal I focused on too often, and I realize I'm not for her. Couples start as friends sometimes, yet even if I'm not allowed to be her boyfriend, we can tend her heart and impart love. I wish to purify my clarity and reasons of why as we continue.

I mustn't cause her to cry anymore. I may remind myself of the door and how some thirst for war; though their desire mustn't be satiated. Some aspire for peace, love, unity, and respect, and it's those people who we best connect. Remember too the qualities of PLU8R are also in the consect.

I saw a webinar with Christy Whitman the day I wrote this paragraph. She teaches seven universal laws, and the one I think of is the law of detachment. I need to release my attachments to some things; like, how I need to release chained dreams. If I remove my projected need to achieve success and allow abundance, sufficiency shall prevail. I can still dream, yet I mustn't affix my self-worth to just accomplishing goals.

Gabby Bernstein also reminds her students not to hound the Universe for the completion of our wishes. I may tell the Universe, God, our higher selves, or even other people my desires, yet if I attach my meaning or worth to achieving them, I could be disappointed. I permit the law of allowance, and since this section is Revelation, I'll share some essential revelations I've had.

The point in time was Fall 2018. I was in school, I had one day a week landscaping, and I was thankful Zeus was living with me. I was also griping how I've done so little. As I settled in, I realized my shift away from promotion and attachment to earnings felt good. I'd also almost completed the final version of the 8th Fountain and was revising *Fragments of Intent* for its final version.

Although I'm only entitled to part of the royalties from my bookwork, a festering idea of prosperity seemed to tell me my books sell. I'm not soliciting for Providing Point like I thought I had to, though I believe the program is valuable. Gathering pledges aren't formed well by pushing the agenda randomly. May we actively engage in marketing in a gradual process?

It sounds like I'm making excuses for not succeeding. What about the concept of removing pressures to perform and just being a decent person? Do I need to be a high performer? Am I settling, giving up, or releasing control to the Universe? Is my faith a passive submission? Or am I releasing an overarching burden from overpromising?

If I release control, then why form these books? If I settle, it could be more comfortable, yet can I find more happiness and contentment anyhow? On the idea of giving up, if I'm sincere, I don't think I put in a great effort at all. I've been overly passive, and if plans are a pathway to life and prosperity, perhaps that's a sign I've *not* done so much.

Spending a few years writing books that few have read, to me, doesn't seem like a worthwhile pursuit. There are intrinsic gains I've made, and some have said I should write books only because I enjoy doing so. Some of the same people too have recommended giving up on thinking they'll expand into anything past a casual interest or hobby.

The process of forming these books draws a bizarre and stylistic weave. After distilling the text, the Unlimited versions of these books form, and I feel an urge to buy copies and share them. By the time the final versions are ready, the post Unlimited copies, I've not yet promoted and asked for purchases from barely anyone. I think, in line with the title of this chapter, that I'm getting clear and confident my writing does hold value for others. I've not always thought that.

I am valuable too and shall attempt to sell books. I've had self-worth issues in the past, and perhaps that's part of this situation since I've not succeeded with sales. If the books are all about me, and I think *I'm* not valuable, why do I leave my ideas and books floating out there?

For the 8th Fountain, I shared the $5 idea of Providing Point, and in my Fall 2018 Global Development Studies (GDS) class, I had a fifty-cent idea. From the course, an ethical twang pinged me about my coffee consumption. The half a dollar idea is about coffee and ethical principles of its production, and I'll share it here.

I'm an avid coffee drinker, and also don't like using people, manipulation, or taking advantage of others. The Global South is the primary producer of coffee, yet I didn't realize how terrible the global situation is regarding coffee.

From the class, I learned that the retail per pound sale price of coffee is substantially overpriced. As a North American, I understood coffee is expensive, yet I didn't know that the base price for pre-roasted coffee is often under $2 a pound. We learned how a Nicaraguan farm considered well off only earned $30k/year for its owners.

I understand and accept that the Global South and 'underdeveloped' countries have a lower GDP and poverty line, though to think a coffee farm of a few many hectares generates only $30,000 as the profit for the owners is surprising.

I feel appalled about the amount of effort and time that goes into picking the beans for such a low wage for the workers. If the workers received $2/pound of selected coffee, it would still be a ridiculously low wage, yet $2 a pound is the price paid for the raw beans *after* production?

I also learned the roasting process isn't as time-consuming as I had thought it was before class; we discovered it takes less than an hour to roast a batch. If a mainstream coffee company buys beans for $2 a pound, cooks them, and then sells coffee for $16 a pound or $2-3 a cup that's a ridiculously high markup.

I grasp the concept it costs money to build stores, pay for overhead, and also to facilitate operations, though from seeing and hearing about coffee farms, it seems that the disparity in earnings is quite high.

A question I asked in the class was 'what would happen if the small farms roasted their beans and sold the roasted coffee directly to the market.' Stephen (the professor) said that they would then have to compete with the larger coffee suppliers. He also laughed out loud when I suggested that the roasted coffee could sell for $11/pound and to use the other $5/pound for distribution.

Though Stephen didn't talk so much in class about fair-trade coffee, I adore the premise of the coffee farmers and their employees getting far more than they are. Stephen also told our class how the $30k/year owners needed protection for their safety.

Perhaps it's my viewpoint from being in the 1st World, a biased point of view, the disparity is too much. Boycotting coffee isn't the pathway either. It would be fantastic for the farmers to earn more, yet how much control do I have as a North American consumer?

Farming coffee is the life and sustenance of the pickers and farm owners, so boycotting coffee isn't a good idea. What I'd like is that the farmers earn much more. If a coffee shop or company needs to cover their costs, I understand that, yet they should not abuse the people who provide the essential product they need to survive as a business.

In class, we heard how coffee has had a fixed price for its raw form. If we double or triple the cost of green bean coffee from $1.50 to $3.00 or even $4.50 a pound, that still seems low, yet it would have a more substantial impact on the farms. If a farm can operate a profit of $1.50 per pound, then $3.00 per pound would be more than a 200% increase in profits. $3.00 per pound still seems far too little for something that the Global North is abusing so covertly.

Wishes and prayers can't 'fix' the situation either. From WorldAtlas.com, Canada is 10th in the world for coffee consumption at 6.5kg per capita per year (Finland is top at 12kg/capita). 6.5kg for 33 million people is 214.5 million kg of coffee. At US$2.80 on the day, 6.5kg is $600 million per year for unprocessed coffee.

I'm a bit twanged that when I pay Starbucks CAD$2.54 for my basic 16-20oz coffee that somewhere along the chain of the bean that a person is spending an entire day combing through a coffee farm/forest with bugs or rain hounding them earning barely enough money even in their whole day to buy that one cup of coffee I drink.

I believe in a basic living wage for people, though I can't understand the feeling of how it is to work full days for so little as a coffee worker. I get that different countries and cultures have different expectations and living standards, and we can compare people like different countries.; the situations and expectations are different between people.

My income was under $24k/year in 2016 and 2017, yet I still feel wealthy. According to Canadian standards, I'm below the poverty line, though I'm also blessed, fortunate, and grateful to have some luxuries and even access to schooling and support.

I've also had access to coffee, cigarettes, food, shelter, and even clean water in a tap in my kitchen!? When people producing the garments we wear and coffee we drink can't even afford food, there may be an issue.

I have a weird thought here, though. What would happen if the coffee producing countries fixed their prices at a much higher rate? What if every coffee-producing farm set their price at over $5 a pound? If the suppliers fixed their prices and demanded more for what they've created, would the coffee companies adjust their behaviours? The GDS professor told us it would mean that the coffee wouldn't be sold and go to rot. That wouldn't be a solution either.

What about the concept of coffee shops collecting or charging a premium that goes directly back to the producers as cash? If a farm is supplying a shop with coffee, then that shop could sponsor that specific farm with collected income and pledges to go directly to the farm.

If a shop collected 50c extra per cup and sold 500 cups a day, that's $250/day. Annually that's $91,250 that could be put directly to improving the farm and paying higher wages. If Stephen's farm example curates $30k/year and is considered successful, $91,250 extra per year for the workers, equipment, and expansion of the farm could be significant.

When I was in high school (a long while ago, in 1996), I thought of the Freestyle Café. I wanted to open an Internet café on Manly Beach in Australia. 1996 was before the Internet took root, though why I think of that now is a seed concept for independent coffee shops.

If a small sized chain of coffee shops is supplied by only one or two specific farms for the entirety of their coffee supply, we could make a kind and cool deal. On the premise of 1,000kg of green beans per hectare of coffee and 1kg producing 125 cups of coffee (8g per cup), using the numbers, it could mean $62.50 per kilogram or $62,500 per

SHARDS OF MY SOUL

hectare to the producers.

What if mainstream chains cut their profits by 50c a cup of brewed coffee and dispense it to the people who are providing for their first world dream spots? Monetary handouts aren't the most fantastic paths or idea, though the compounded math stuns me a bit.

If companies have stronger coffee with even 16g or 20g per cup making, that's 50 cups per kg. A 50c levy per cup could put $25 per kg back to the people who produce coffee beans. I'm not sure if the idea is comprehendible or logical, though expand the concept. My profit mind sees the numbers of what's possible with direct coffee production and wonders if it can be activated.

In my paper, I saw the 1,000kg per hectare, 125 cups per kg, plus the 50c idea per cup to math into valuing a baseline. A profit or financial focus cruxed into my mind with the entrepreneurial concept of "If $62,500 per hectare can be earned on 50c a cup, then how could the land be bought?"

Rewind to the in-class reaction though. Owners of farms are not earning anywhere near $62.5k on farms more than a hectare. Why not? If mainstream coffee places sell a 16oz coffee for $2.50, they need to cover overhead and other expenses, though what would happen if they recalled even half the 50 cents; 25 cents per cup of coffee?

If companies put 25c back to the farms, then even if at 50 cups per kilo, $12.50 could be reimbursed to the farms as a kind thank you and reward for providing us with the super kind luxury and 1st World drug upon which we've become reliant.

I checked the web for the business name Grower's Direct Coffee; someone else held the name. The company declared bankruptcy in 2013, though what if someone could get ahold of the title and rights and start this idea up?

My $5 plan for the Fraser Valley hadn't yet sprouted, and I wanted to find my pathway to income that is non-governmental. Perhaps a win/win could be seen in the coffee market? A small café could sprout to hold a place for gathering locally, and what would happen if part of the earnings went back to the growers? T'is an idea, and I think it might be fair.

RATIONALIZATION

I felt tentative, fragile, and dumb at the moment I first typed this. The energy of resilience and self-induced pressure, though, extended the cursor across the page. I had yet to write the repentance chapter, yet this one includes further revelations.

I'm not prepared for life. I'm not very strong and feel delicately placed in my home. Some criticize millennials for being snowflakes, yet I've felt even less sturdy than that. This fountain is in the Fountains of Fortitude, and in line with the comment about building a house on sand, it seems like I'm constructing a future on the water.

I laughed at this point because I carry humour with me as a coping mechanism; it helps release neurosis. "I'm on a boat!" Thank you all for letting me cruise along these streams of text that wish to assure the waters are clean and vital for life.

It was a Wednesday and in Survivor season when I started this chapter, and the bodacious dream of competing lingered that night after hearing a speech. Kerian is a Toastmaster, and his message that night was how we need to do difficult and challenging things to strengthen ourselves. If I can make it to the point of refining the silt to clay, I'd love to be put into the Survivor fire to set like clay in a kiln.

Once established, sure, and secure, pottery fired in a kiln can hold the waters of life as a vessel for others. I wish we abound with grace, kindness, and generosity, yet I also want to have the grit, confidence, and determination to be a solid, sure, and secure male. My age says I'm an adult, though I still feel like I'm just a child and not a man.

Dad doesn't understand my desire to compete on the show, and I very well make a fool of myself and not reach the merge, yet a weird and wild twist nudges me to believe it's part of the journey. It may be to prove some things to myself, part of it may be fantasy, and a portion of competing also is because I see Survivor as a rite of passage.

Thinking about my relationship status, I know most women don't want to go out with a man-child. Regarding a lack of confidence, it spills not only from the cup of not being a contributing, employed, and valued member of society, though also to the fact I've not been able to provide for myself, let alone a girlfriend or wife.

It's stunning that I'm still alive. I'm forty years old and still feeling as if I'm a child. When I call myself a child to my Mom, she tells me, "you're forty, you're an adult!" though I honestly don't feel like that. It almost feels like I'm getting younger as the moments press me forward to infinity. And yet at some points, I feel like I've been around forever.

There are some great things about feeling like I'm a child and not a man. I can be silly and playful sometimes, happy to be a fool, and I also can remind myself that forever, I can know what it's like to be meek, safe, and loved. Maybe my immaturity is a coping mechanism for fear, though it's also an outlet for happiness and play.

If I think that I'm just a kid, though, there's no understandable way to think I could ever achieve what I set out to do in the earlier Fountains. There is no way my previous dreams can manifest unless I find courage and faith to be an adult and get diligent with my work.

Even when writing these books, I'm not clear they are putting in work. Achieving the accomplishment of printing eight or so books up to now doesn't even sink into my self-worth, sometimes, I've thought my purpose, my meaning, and my worth is dependent upon the success of the books and Providing Point. Since neither was yet thriving, I deemed myself a failure.

If I release the dreams of profitable authorship and success regarding pledges, the work very well could be a complete waste. I've thought that. Here, again, though, I'm on the computer putting the books together and pushing onwards with bizarre intangible belief.

Am I rationalizing this to deny any responsibility for my actions? No. Am I explaining my essential failure as an excuse not to work? Not quite. Even if I put the Patreon page on hold instead of closing it, does the reason I didn't close it signify my belief is the program shall still thrive? I'm not certain.

What I am sure of, though, is I *am* a fool, *and* I don't want to rationalize. Reverting to the first Fountain's topic, Natalie, I don't think I could even look her in the eyes. If I submit to the universe and fate, is it quitting, or allowing the channels to be what they naturally shall be?

Chandra had just called. Because I removed chapters about her and Magic codes from Fragments of Intent, referring to the systems wouldn't make sense to people even if they've read everything available. I also remember that I'd not yet included the allocation information for *Open to Fate,* the 8th Fountain.

Open to Fate's revenues go to a local street mission in Chilliwack called Ruth and Naomi's. Ruth and Naomi's helps on street level providing shelter and food for people who need such. For *Sand to Silt,* 100% of its profits go to Water.org, and I rewind to earlier in this chapter; how I've been building a house on the water.

"One who lives in a glass house should not throw stones."

Very accurate, yet what about glass-bottomed boats? Dare we look down to the realms below, or reach up to the heavens and stretch high into the sky like an inverted abyss?

My Dad suggested I write a book of rhymes, though he didn't know I already have one forming. The book is called *Shared Node,* and bizarrely, I think the book may be a good read. It's only part-way done, though lingers as a creative project.

With my writing, I've thought I'm to be an author as my profession, though I'm not clear that I am. I contradict that by working on this book, and though I see many contradictions in my life, I have thought I've known what my purpose is.

Some other names surface in my consciousness that I push out and away because I think they are people I shouldn't focus on again. There's that word; *shouldn't.* I italicize it to stress the importance of the idea that I believe it projects. Because I think I *shouldn't* think of some things, doing so denies part of my heart. I also best mention some crucial people.

The School of Greatness with Lewis Howes is formational as a podcast and person to learn from. I wrote Lewis a chapter in the 3rd Fountain though deleted it from *Fragments of Intent.* Natalie Imbruglia is another name that's calls even though I've thought she wishes I never knew her name or who she is. Starting by writing to her is how this entire series of books and creative expedition began.

The third primary, Gary Vaynerchuk, coaxes me to work because I'm dramatically lazy and unproductive. My self-reflection and atonement by working on the Fountains hold the books aren't valuable if no one read them. No matter what the words of the book carry, my pathway of writing for others and promising to give from future sales is what I follow through with.

Best I now presume, even if I don't entirely believe it, that these books *are* a waste of time and I'm a slacker? Though I've written books, I still know I've been lazy. Writing these books is not too difficult a process, and also, if I learn from them, their revision and reformation are valuable.

Reworking and revising the books draw me from points of insanity into a severe questioning of 'why am I doing this?' This existential doubt happens when I write sometimes, yet writing is a fantastic learning channel. Whatever I wish, whatever I hope, whatever I seem to think is my purpose, I rewind it up to the hands of fate and destiny.

Releasing attachment to Earth is a thing I'm concerned about as I fear I'll slip off this planet if I don't have a purpose. That may be part of my drive. I've written this before, though I may need to repeat it to myself. "Rob! Don't *push* for the purpose; *have a* purpose!"

But what happens if I think my purpose is death and I'm

being used for massive unity; a unifying bond to end me? I've wished to unify people, though I want to work *with* people. These books are created mostly when alone, yet can their distribution and dissemination be part of a positive inclusion I can also live with cohesively?

It was Halloween night 2018 a week before I was this far into my work. I had a speech at Toastmasters, and it was surprisingly successful. I presented a talk titled *A Wizard's Brew* about *Camellia Sinensis*; tea. The twist was I was dressed in a long grey robe and spoke in the tone of a wizard.

I presented with a voice of deep resonance and an alternate personality, and through writing and practicing the speech, I went a bit crazy by enacting the character. One thing I learned, though, was the value of using a variety of sound to fragment and hone my words.

Another voice I've tried a bit is the sergeant; an army person's tone of voice. One thing I like about the sergeant is his attitude towards Zeus. The wizard had spoken harshly to the cat, yet the sergeant loves him and speaks super kindly. There's dear affection for Zeus from the sergeant while the wizard was put off by there being a cat in his home.

I've also sometimes feared my consciousness is hijacked when it seems like people have learned my pathways and predictability. Some then have imitated me and misguide me to points of negative thought. I need to align my heart with my mind, and then let my soul build spirit. We each have our bodies, and I hope we know they're not all we are.

I wrote about the five different parts of being in the 4th Fountain, yet I also alluded to the various forms of self in *Fragments of Intent*. The multiple types of person sourced from a Human Services class where they taught us there are four: the open self, the blind self, the hidden self, and the unknown self.

I expanded the theory to include the perceived self, the conscious self, the nodal self, the perceptual self and the recorded self. If we weave concepts in a cross-modal fashion, we could align all these forms of person to the Fountains. When I cross-reference things by affixing a shared or correlated meaning, though, it can cause unrest or jostle consciousness. Think too, though, of the reflected self.

"Clarity of each word makes sense to the bird."

I'm a mere human, and my path isn't always clear. I've not always been confident, and I accept I have a consequence. If implications are part of the equation, it matters how we open up to the future, and I don't know if to close the past with forces of worlds to share words.

We might open a lost key, yet still, I wonder if we see the thorns cleared and remove the psychic debris. As I navigate the course of these texts successfully, we find a few who were lost at sea. Webs of excuses fuse my being into how I don't understand what to do as cryptic currency reminds us of the loom and facts of the pace we presume. I allude to tomorrow, though we don't know what tomorrow holds yet as a lived reality.

Is it always wise to envision and plan for the future? When I lack faith and trust in living and imagining good things, fear has often clouded my hopes and vision. I'm hesitant to guess or predict the future. In January 2017, I aimed for a goal of selling 15,000 books by August that year, and up to this book's release, thirteen Amazon copies had sold.

Was it my lack of faith and belief that caused me not to achieve the goal? Perhaps. Had I set an unrealistic goal? I think so. I may have been working with wishful, not optimistic, thinking. I certainly didn't do what I needed to do to achieve selling thousands of copies by August 2017.

I've also sought gain without getting my heart and spirit deep into work. I've been lax and not attempted to attain my core dreams; those that have maybe driven me insane. With recalibration and a shift in my work, I hope to again bring valuable seeds into our fields and gardens.

"Grain by grain, row by row.
Sometimes flowers need time to grow."

REPARATIONS

If we need to reassess, regather, and restart, then so it is. If we're to make up for the mistakes we make, we must make a conscious choice to do so too. I must atone for my mistakes, to make reparations, yet that part is what I'm doing by writing these books and this chapter.

My mother visited November 10th, 2018. She and my Dad have cared well for me for many years, and I wish to reciprocate by succeeding. My books, ideas, and pitches are to achieve a life where I may be the provider, not the one supported. If I'm allowed prosperity, I'll be able to provide even more.

Reparations can be considered a combination of repentant positive reciprocation and action. I'm aware I've lived with extreme amounts of grace, fortunate circumstances, and support, and in repayment to the world, I think I must write more. We don't know how or if the Fountains can be a commercial success, yet as intents hone skills and promises, we evolve myself and how I behave.

Sometimes we can't communicate with those with whom we wish to make reparations. Even if we repent to God or Allah or the Universe, we may want to make direct contact with the ones we've wronged. Some humans are forgiving, and some we may have affected negatively or unjustly may have forgotten about us entirely or not forgive.

When we make a mistake with someone, we may wish to make up for it right away; partly that's what people are doing when they engage in damage control. If we make a mistake, sometimes we may not be forgiven, though. We can learn how to act and behave differently in the future, though, and changing our behaviours can prevent us from making the same transgressions again.

If a person resents us, or even if many do, we may want to

make reparations. Is that so *we* feel okay again? In some cases, it's also a layer of self-preservation as a motive. If people hold a grudge we intuit or sense, saying sorry isn't always enough. Remember too that not all people shall tell us when we've wronged them; we may not even know they're offended.

Our reasons for *why* we behaved a certain way may not even matter to others. It is the reaction and feelings of another that matter, and they may not care or consider our intents. When our reasons aren't clear if we trigger strong emotions, the 2nd R of PLU8R says we must be responsible. It may be a responsibility to forgive others too if they wrong us.

Many variables are similar between humans, yet we're all explicitly and distinctly different people with entirely different perspectives. Understanding multiple perspectives and people can open our minds and hearts, yet if we make a mistake, we know things can change near instantaneously.

People don't all have the same ethical standards or philosophies as us. If we are to be conduits for grace, compassion, and forgiveness, we can remind ourselves we're flawed humans too. If it's in our heart and mind to improve lives around us, then it's best to believe in forgiveness to receive and share it.

Being alone, I must remember that there's an entire world out there beyond myself. Even if I think I'm on my own, countless lives are carrying on with people feeling a full range of emotions. The diversity of passion and experience is so vast we may not comprehend.

I still must make reparations, though. My mind is one of the best, worst, and most important parts of my being. Ideas are easy to manipulate and make mistakes with, and even if I feel remorse for mistaken thoughts, sometimes damage can't be corrected or reversed.

I must make a shift back to responsibility; if I'm to be a global citizen and a local community member, I must unify my true intents of heart with my mind to be in cohesion. Since I've had issues in the past, and even recently, I know there may be some people to whom I need to make reparations.

I've endured through significant negative feelings, terrible thoughts, and emotional debris, and I've felt terrified, irritated, and insecure while delicately placed in my home. I remember reparations are not always pleasant, and though I wish to atone, some people may never forgive.

I also remember we can't expect others to do, say, or think the way we want them to. There is a variety of moral issues, values, and ethics, and thought it would be fantastic to have all people kind, loving, forgiving, and generous. That's not entirely rational, though.

We need to find those to love and trust that are okay to interact and communicate, and as I've been isolated and alone, I remember I'm the one who needs to make reparations. I must correct the misgivings, errors, and transgressions and activate PLU8R in myself for other people.

If I can't or won't control other people, then I must grab hold of the wheel that guides my soul and charts a particular course. Truth, divinity, and sanctity hold firm as we navigate the waters of life while some come from a place of death that wish to bring life. Angels and some passed on still hold power on Earth in our hearts, minds, and souls, while some spirits hold the demons at bay.

I yearn to evade concern and turn how I burn the ciggies into how they help me learn. Do we find kind birds cross the sky to tell us why? Can we allow the plow to now show the text that protects us in communities and consects?

It's a wish, prayer, and hope that we may live decades further into the future together on Earth, and I can't change all the bad things of the world. I can, though, hone myself to improve and be better than I have been.

Construction of our lives and text are what the next three Fountains are. The Fountains form a penance, partly, and are an exploration and exposition of my thoughts. There is an amplification of consciousness and hearts assisted too, as reading these books helps radiate our feelings. Thank you for doing so.

Are the scary feelings a sense of a retaliation others are

attempting to make? Maybe. What is the driving force behind these works? Obsession. We elude a definite primary purpose that needs to commandeer these words into the hands of readers.

Are these books quarries of text that hold valuable insights? They may be. Will readers find others also to dig up and mine them? I didn't yet know. If I have given some of the work aside to fate, shall people open the texts? My hope is, yes.

My intuition tells me that many shall read these books, yet why are such momentous and profound energies found in me when I write? I wrote how writing them is simple enough, yet at some points, they are dangerously tricky to form. My psychosis is part of who I am, and some may never comprehend the mind-frame.

Perseverance to write and shape these books can't precisely say how they're worth something though. If effort compounds, can we imagine the future blessings that come from their creation? I can. The reparations I make are putting my life into the hands of God and letting The Universe guide me towards the chords of divinity.

There may be a split between a self-derived income and accepting support from significant sources, yet I put trust in God and The Universe. Some writers channel and download information from their mind into the keys, and perhaps that's a writing style to use in the future.

Dear God, please help me find pathways and areas of peace to live within. The consect does not seem a safe place, and I feel that my placement in it is in Your intents. Please grant me courage, faith, strength, truth, trust, and hope to excel and thrive and not just cope. Amen

.

It's clear now. Get to work, continue to learn, develop, and understand, and continue to write and form these books. I need to market my work and generate awareness, pledges, and interest in Providing Point.

I'd not gotten to writing so much about Providing Point yet in this Fountain, yet the process is in action. Reading the book gives me faith, hope, and trust that my work is consumed. It was December 3rd, 2018. The day held my last English class for the year and the completion of my group project for Global Development Studies.

My atonement forms. Gathering pledges and sales earn for the causes we assist, yet pulls of uniting people, resources, and sanity is tricky. Maybe some would love to read my books and buy them, yet don't know about their existence. There may be people who know about Providing Point and are on the fence about giving a pledge. Real conversations and understanding the program may be what's required.

What if I need to suspend my belief to attune the fact that some people would love to support with a purchase or pledge? As I get past my feeling that promotion is awkward or uncomfortable, I shift to understanding people matter, and I need to know what to provide to give value.

The Introversial prerogative is to learn, love, live, thrive, create, play and pray, and it's a helpful guidepost on this journey. I continue to learn and evolve, and I must remember to love and care generously and genuinely. As we lighten up and release our fears and insecurities, we may live and thrive even more. The 'create, play, and pray' parts are also meant to be enjoyable and not merely penance.

I learn a great deal from heeding other authors and artists and what they've written or said too. Though working on the Fountains carry a necessity for me to work and grow, we evolve and change intents, actions, and awareness to allow shared prosperity. You, as a reader, give an impetus to create.

When this was forming, I didn't know how to sell thousands of copies of these books, and I may need to structure my plans, and even my thoughts, to focus on creating quality work. It must be worthwhile for readers and not just because of potential earnings.

I call for faith to guide. As each selected letter directs the text, I ask the consects and communities guide with subtle hints. There also are the one-hour recordings *Shared Node* on Ambispheric's *Masters of Drum and Bass Vol. 22* and *Sediment of*

Intent on Fluidified's *Illusions of Existence* to share. The lyrics source from the Contialis and are also part of this involution.

When I start books, they often call for completion. An obsessive tendency guides this work, and as the world nudges me to do the right things for the right reasons, I'm thankful and humbled by the grace given.

Though I hadn't yet started to earn much of anything with books and music, we had gained the first seven patrons by February 2019. Am I doing the right things? Let me be doing so, please. When I find myself doing the right or correct things, though, I've also wanted to be clear as to *why* I am doing them and what they are.

This Fountain formed slowly. The weight of previous work and energy reminded me editing books hone my abilities and craft further. Compounded lessons, skills, ideas, and purposes nudge insecurities away while I'm aware the Fountains are so much *about* me, yet they're not just *for* me. The work is for *our* future of which, yes, mine is a part. I desire to learn to speak, share, and guide with care and heart.

So while this chapter took a while to write, the process of forming the Fountains continues.

RESTORATION

The definitions of restoration from Google are:

1. The action of returning something to a former owner, place, or condition.
2. The return of a hereditary monarch to a throne, a head of state to government, or a regime to power.

A life calls the walled confines of my being. Seeing the truth of our youth, we call back to how then is now. I've said some things so often, yet even I've not believed it's the love we receive, I solemnly and hopefully sip my drink.

You made your vows, and I believed you would keep them. I'd thought I lost you without ever having seen your real face in person, yet during parts of the day I formed this, I thought of how we're living. If Heaven is a real place, I pray those who landed there can help keep us safe.

Some may jest or think I live in a castle, though don't forget about the homes and halls of our heart. The worlds of the past and distant future have worked through me before, and though I've not heard the songs of the future, I hope we may create more.

Our souls may need to express and share, even if fame isn't the goal. Natalie became famous, though was that what she wanted? I've also seen videos of Gary Vaynerchuk recently that show dozens of people lining up to give him a hug, a handshake, or a thank you. I'm not sure I'd like to be famous like that. Super fame is not the goal. I intend to have an audience base large enough to facilitate a goal of 3,000 books or albums sold per month.

If I sell books, it's true that people shall know me and who I am, though I don't need millions in sales. A friend recommended I use a pen-name to hide my identity, yet I don't.

I have, though, hidden so many thoughts, feelings, and words in the tracks. How can we restore my mind and soul to the actual beliefs of love and respect I hold.

My cat has been amazing to me. Zeus was who I wrote to in the first section of *Sand to Silt*, yet the date I wrote this, I was called back to *Finding Natalie*, the first Fountain. Some have been through massive amounts of sadness, distrust, and perhaps even disgust, and I cannot ask to remove feelings from memory. I also don't want to seed future misgivings and lies.

I felt a pain below my heart that tells me I've sunk low. To think of Natalie twenty years after we haven't met openly in person, I kindly tell myself that I don't know her or who she is other than an imagined spirit. We won't know what the truth is until her and I meet.

At this point, my Dad filtered into my thoughts. He told me to never think of Natalie while many others in the world have also told me not to do so. My mind gets in and out of the way of what love is. Sometimes it calls crystal clarity to say she and I are soulmates, and other times intuition tells me the romance isn't real. I hoped, wished, and prayed to meet her, yet some things seem to fade away.

Perhaps I'm right, or maybe many other things get in the way confusing the truth. Just because I think I've loved Natalie, it doesn't mean I always believe it. No one needs to know how my unidirectional obsession shares the context.

I don't know what the future holds, and if it's best to write about what we know, it may be a reason why I've not written so much about us. I've not been excellent at learning and understanding other people and their lives, though if I want to support people with their lives, I need to know about them too.

There can be a truth about knowing general parameters or outer knowledge and sharing with people, and working on ourselves can change us, sometimes. If to connect with the core of another person, we must learn to understand them too. A relationship is how others relate to ourselves also and not just what we alone think and feel.

I can't tell you who you are. I can't always tell you why I behave the way I do either. I can, though, be a conduit of understanding to expose our thoughts openly. By doing so, some people may read and find new information, insights, or parallels about how we are on Earth.

Sometimes I keep myself in check to assure I can act, behave, and produce ethically. I've not always done so, though some things I keep from doing because I know they could ruin me. I need to increase my respect, explore my insecurities, and share my genuine feelings and reasons more often.

Women & Songs 2, track three. It is fair; it's best I don't say "I love you" so often. What's more crucial and vital is to know what I shall do without proclaiming it — a kind reminder that I do without explicitly telling you.

With the definition of restoration as returning something to a former owner, place, or condition, I must do some things. Regarding one released to God, I think of what they left behind. Many people loved and liked the person, though we know they can't come back.

We know when another has died, they are gone from Earth. For us, I'm glad we've not left, and I feel sad and thankful we're still orbiting the sun. We're on this planet with some that reset the chances of fate and destiny to meet.

Although the next chapter is Repentance, I've prayed PLU8R often in the same sequence as this book's chapter titles. Perhaps repentance is shared too late, yet if we can genuinely cycle through every point perhaps the order matters. Are the words in order because they deepen the importance of repentance?

If the words of PLU8R cycle, mix, and interchange, shall we mix all the words and worlds into the brew of respect to renew? Renewal of our mind, emotions, and feelings can be beneficial, yet we may need to pass through the full cycle to reach that point. Is it best for us for me to be before the keyboard typing these pages, or put onto communal stages?

Think of the friends you've known and from whom you've strayed. Perhaps there could be a restoration in those friendships too. If we've kept me away from some because of projected beliefs, the thoughts reveal I'm not always accurate and have mislabeled others without real recognition.

Some shards are contialitic guards that may be against us, and though some are aligned against me, we restore the revealed truth to dissipate their hate. Is calling out about misgivings accusation or revealing? I ask we let intents guide our official recognition and make admission to the moment of now. I remind us we find The Spirit kind.

For those who've passed on from Earth, you left some behind who need to continue without you. Some here know you left tears waving along the shoreline calling out for hope; a hope they forgive us for not knowing what to do for you. I feel remorse for the truth you didn't want Earth to keep you.

Earth does keep us, yet we must accept some lessons are not pleasant. What do you hope we learn? Can restoration of love, truth, and kindness forge us anew? I don't want to think about how some are gone and cannot be restored to life, and if we feel grief, how can others expect us to be happy?

Grief and layers of forever stack upon the lives we live. I know I can't bring people back from the dead, and I think of three people I knew who died in 2018. We can't resurrect people and, as being alive, we know we can't reverse time. Such things incline me to think of the word reverence as an R-word too.

"Live forever and a day past tomorrow today."

A lesson learned when I wrote this chapter was acceptance. We may feel uncomfortable feelings and not like our situations. Recognition is also learning to be okay in that discomfort. What we must know is even if we don't like things, though accept them, we also can choose what to do past the point of acceptance.

I was feeling grief the day I wrote this. I accept we can't change the facts of what is, and though I may feel uncomfortable and woeful, we must endure. Our world has lost many influential people, and loss can be devastating. I've not dealt with much loss in my life, so grief isn't something I'm used to feeling. I want to learn how to comfort people, though also hope I don't have to acquire the skill through future losses.

Some friends care and love so much, and knowing that they feel so profoundly is humbling and a kind reminder that people do love, care and cherish thoroughly. Space's traces of human life hold us here in our souls. I wish we may thrive and that the nets cast into our view bring us closer.

We hold a pressure sensitive way to live, keeping us in time's sieve. The rhymes may give me into temptations of chemical pleasure, yet the directive to thrive allows us to grow. I can't take away some feelings, though my responsibility is to add, shape and mould some sands of eternity.

How does Heaven tend tomorrow? If we're always in the moment of now, how shall we be there in the arms of the angels calling Earth to host their love? By remembering them now, even if we'd not seen these words until a few months, or even years, later, the Fountains flourish as a processing journal.

Much of my life is irrelevant to most, yet I have to remind myself these books are for those that love and care. There are activations of Earthly objectives wound through the process of working on these books, and even if few have drawn in the intents and sands, the cultivation of soul holds how I keep applying to enroll.

I shall not give up, I believe in more than a few, and I also hold onto my dreams. Continue to learn to speak with heart and clarity as somehow the whys assist how to rise.

I sometimes prefer to work solitary in the nighttime while Zeus and I are living in our apartment. I value friends, family, and those we know, and even if I'm afraid to put my toes in the waters of life, the words of this Fountain condense. We intermingle with spiritual alignment, and we work for many; some work for all and all may need to know the subtle union of the flow.

I'm called to the restoration of my responsibility to tend

these books. I hope you may share them, expand their reach, and gain from reading them. I've seen how some people want to connect, and I'm glad and thankful I don't have too much attention. I'm not wanting millions of followers or having people at me every second of every day jostling for attention.

I want to earn money, yes, though I want to talk to groups and relish in the luxury of having time on my own. Instead of having massive amounts of fame, broad sweeps and wishes of hope remind me I'm fortunate not to be massively exposed to millions of people.

People have told me multiple times it shouldn't matter that I've not yet reached a broad audience. I understand selling thousands of books can open me up further to the public eyes and ears, and I accept that. I also don't know how it happens.

Many years ago, I wanted to perform lyrics on stage and be an artist. In the past years, I'm thankful that I don't need to play shows or cater to the wants of a record label, and weirdly, it's kind of cool to be creative without having thousands of screaming fans.

And yet a tug calls on my chest that I need to get myself further out there. Glacially this work forms. I don't know if I should tempt the hands of fate by pushing my bookwork and instead think of the gathering concept. If we can continue to create and form these books and gradually grow an audience and pledges, it might save us from massive expansion and overwhelm.

I learn how to deal with mass exposure slowly and not by getting tossed into the blender of fame. Step by step, drip-by-drip, we walk into the ocean and future without drowning.

It was Christmas evening 2018, and the books I had open in mid-read were *#AskGaryVee* by Gary Vaynerchuk, *True Refuge* by Tara Brach, and *This is Marketing* by Seth Godin. I had finished *The Mask of Masculinity* by Lewis Howes the previous week, and it was only a month or so previously that I completed *Quantum Success* by Christy Whitman.

I also recommended *Own Your Own Mind* by Napoleon Hill to a friend and had peeked into the Bible on a rare occasion. I finished Steve Jobs' biography by Walter Isaacson as books are some of the seeds I heed. For having access to them, I'm thankful.

Seth's book about marketing was the most alluring when I wrote this, and thinking about Providing Point as a business made me understand it's best. I learn how to sell. I also must remember that marketing is different than only advertising. It's about expanding awareness, isn't just asking for money, and is about forming s community around an idea to improve collective and personal situations.

The turn of New Years holds a crucial point of time for each of us. Marie Forleo gave three questions to answer about the previous year. First is "what did we do, accomplish, or experience in the year that we're proud of?" Second, "what were some of our biggest mistakes, and what did we learn from them?" And thirdly, "what are we willing to release from the previous year?"

I was proud of releasing a few Fountains books in 2018, for living through another year, and finding and keeping some contacts that I like and love. The mistake I made was trying to do too much on my own and giving too much without sustainability; I need to build slowly, trust my intuition, and trust the process. I also release my need to act or behave only for my benefit, and I release chasing and seeking people who don't reciprocate or want me to contact.

New Year's resolutions may not be relevant at the moment you read this, though I add an idea. Use a word to signify the entire year as your intent for that year.

2018 for me was happiness, and through the Christmas holidays, my heart was profoundly full and heavy. The joy wasn't always there during 2018, though near the close of the year, I thought my happiness and joy are to fortify and solidify for the next year's layered foundation; love.

REPENTANCE

The responsibility for my life should not be placed on others who are not willing. If I want to earn my way in life, I must make substantial changes to how I've been living. I need to maintain my promises, I must find income that is not from taxpayers or people who don't want to support me, and I must reknit my prerogatives and philosophies into the fabric of who I am.

I've been living freely, and I also must honour and acknowledge those who have allowed me to do so. I'd pushed away many friends and contacts because of asking for sales and pledges even while not generating many of either. I value others beyond a purchase or being a patron, though my projected thoughts tell me people avoid contact because I've made requests.

It might be I need to make reparations and personal repentance, not just secular repentance by dredging up all of my faults and errors. Regret is a feeling; our feelings of guilt, shame, or remorse partly are what repentance is. Repentance also is shifting away from continuously making similar transgressions as for what we're repentant.

Must all of our mistakes and misgivings be brought up to public light so that we may absolve ourselves of guilt? What if revealing and admitting mistakes and errors lead to strong condemnation? We may repent, though what if others judge us harshly? Perhaps repentance is best just to God in prayer and not open like a foolish exposition, or is that me fearing to admit faults openly?

Another view could be that shock value could even sell a book or yet make things worse. Writing repentance to solicit attention could amplify adverse effects and isn't a pathway I follow. Writing the truth is vital and crucial; I value honesty, yet I also fear acceptance.

Maybe it's that fear of not being accepted that chains my insecurities. It wouldn't be logical for me to expect all people to approve of me for who I am; that could be very naïve thinking. Some tell us, though, that we shouldn't worry about what others think. Much of my work *has* been striving to be accepted and appreciated by an audience.

Many of the ideas and wants in this book require a larger group of people to approve and activate some of what forms. I mustn't expect people to accept or follow blindly. For who I am and what I do, and from the results in my personal life up to now, I wonder if it's what I've done that has pushed almost everyone away.

If I repent to God and receive salvation, is it because He controls all things, and people, and also forgives me?

I've been having difficulty with the concept of God. I've cognitively understood the social saving power of Jesus though don't act or behave the way an active believer would. I think of other Christians and how judgmental some can be with how they behave — having a large group of people hardline believing in something that I don't entirely devote myself to mixes my concerns.

I wish not to preach or proclaim something in which I'm not wholly confident, and a separate issue in line with repentance is I don't understand how I can activate Providing Point. I've found concerns about the program's structure and see places where it makes sense to adjust. I have a fear it may not be the right thing, even if mostly for the right reasons. Note there, *mostly* for the right reasons.

If I don't believe entirely in the program, then why pursue it? If I have concerns about broad expansion and the integrity of the program, I also have a bullish faith and trust. Providing Point can make a positive and significant change.

The world has cared for me so amazingly well and, in fairness, I want to support others too. I don't always like how I've relied so much on other sources, and I want to earn my income. I *am* appreciative of having additional support through the recursive issues twisting and spiralling in these texts make me wonder about how and why to continue with the Fountains after this one is complete. Perhaps it's time to shift to a different pathway or a different style and form of work?

Contrary to the title of this chapter, I'd also like to acknowledge some of what I've done right. I've endured through the writing process to reach releasing quite a few books, I started gathering for Providing Point in Chilliwack, and I have maintained all gathered is appropriately shared.

We've found some people to provide, though shall more pledge in the future? I've put in the nights, hours, and days to form these books and have tended some needs while also sharing, and I've also kept at other non-Fountain books from time to time slowly preparing them.

Where I need to improve is clear to me, though. I need to build genuine relationships, release my view that marketing is advertising and push promoting, and get myself to do more of what I earnestly want to do. I need to continue to read, process, and learn, and I need to find other channels and creative outlets to evolve past the first Fountain's wishes.

My intent a few months ago was to write the next three Fountain books, yet I also must heed the results of the first ones. It seems people generally don't want to read what I've written, so do I turn back to music and rhymes or keep at it with the books?

Shared Node is another project, though market viability may be an issue with it too. It was a few months away from release, though the book fueled my second one-hour recording in 2018. By the time *Shards of My Soul* is released, it'll be near the end of May 2019, and we'll have lived through almost half of a year past January 1st, 2019. Much can happen in that timeframe, and I hope to make correct choices to move into a positive future for the remainder of 2019.

I've been prone to forecast or share my wishes, yet shall not at this juncture. Instead, I'll return to how we know there is much I've promised and proclaimed which I've not yet provided. I told people I'll house others with my book earnings and provide on street level, yet haven't however sheltered a single person. I've talked a lot, and considering how much I speak, perhaps its best I close my mouth and keyboard from making new promises.

Let's run through some of my faults. I've displayed a lack of self-control and have relied on others to provide for me. I've talked so much about myself and what I want to talk about without keeping entire interest in people's lives and issues. I've neglected people and stepping up for others when they need help, and I've not paid attention to people when they need a person to talk to or a kind word.

I've focused on my books without getting my hands and heart deep in the dirt to dig up the courage to be myself. I've solicited sympathy and guilt offerings instead of providing value and earning support. I've spent the past two or three years playing in the mud instead of using the past three years to actualize and authentically advocate for people who need a home, food, water, and love.

I've disrespected society by not working full-time on anything, even my dreams and wishes, I've been deep in my chemical addictions without thinking of their consequences, and I could be far more patient, kind, and honest than I have been. I've also been vulgar, abusive, and reactive, I've over spoken and obsessed about my work, thoughts, and process, and I've even rhymed obsessively and haven't listened to or been quiet for others.

I've focused on myself feeling okay and secure instead of being sensitive and caring, I've not learned when to speak up when it's my time to speak, and I've not stood up for others when they're treated unjustly. I've received grace while being slyly critical of others, I've *tried* to be open and honest of my shortcomings, though seemingly secluded my sins by not repenting to God. I've abused my creative freedom of creating anything I want to while staying trapped in set patterns, I've used other people's lyrics without representing them, and I've hidden behind names when I get insecure.

With psychic attention, I've left some entirely untended to

when running into or away from the next moments. I've tried to be original and exciting while used as a beacon conveying nonsense instead of vital and essential information.

I've also revealed some secrets of others and haven't kept confidentiality. I've gossiped a bit and talked about others while manipulating my thoughts to stay sane, and I've also put unwanted attention and focus on people who wish I'd leave them entirely alone.

It continues.

I've talked about love, luck, and life while not putting other people's needs first. When tending other's input and advice, I've not always respected their wisdom too, and I've neglected that others have a right to speak their truths. I've also taken for granted, and sometimes even have gotten mad at, the very few people who call or care for me.

I've also projected and presumed malicious intent from others with no absolute proof, I've focused on my work and obsessed without tending to others, and in rare cases, I've given up with hope or expectation of positive reciprocation.

If we think of benefiting instead of providing for its intrinsic nature, it's not so great. It's best to give without any expectations, and it isn't anyone's responsibility or obligation to provide us with thanks. I've put trust in God to honour with this work. When I've been critical of organized religion at times and thought judgmental ideas and not trusted some who are part of the church, I've put my faith in God and the Universe and shall diligently strive to provide.

Some people give in action and attention to reciprocate my correct respect and homage. I thank them. I too, though, have been critical and biased towards my species for activities I've also committed. Though I've twisted false mirrors and tried to apply truth, I don't know what the facts are and have made comments that sting when I'm guilty of the same accusations. I still have a lot of growing up to do.

I don't even know how or if I'll ever be there and able to cover the needs of my parents when they are 80+ years old. I've not been able to support myself, and I remind myself I've not sought out extra time with my parents because of my resistance to them paying. My parents have blatantly helped me without me being able to reciprocate.

Trips to visit with my parents would be fantastic; though because I project I'm too expensive a child already, I have no idea, clue, or concept about how we can meet. Could I ever be a parent? It still seems I'm not just an only child, yet only a child.

I may be too accepting and not pushing for good things because I'm fearful. Sometimes I think I'm a burden, yet the most prominent thing or issue to repent is that I've not worked full-time and had almost given up on a cause I don't feel an entire passion for pursuing.

I've been reluctant and skeptical on the street because I know I'm not homeless, street, or hardcore and I've projected that the world wants me gone. It sometimes feels like I've made far too many proclamations and open wishes without backing up those claims with concerted effort, heart, and care.

There may be value in the books and Providing Point, though I've not held full faith in activating the program or expecting miracles to happen. Without putting in the effort and seeds needed for them to manifest, I give my repentance.

I feel remorse for my wrongdoing and sin, though perhaps those feelings are also something I need to accept and release. With negative emotions, maybe it's good to feel them and to acknowledge them. I feel exhausted from the past few years writing books, and that may be why I've not formed so much new material in the past few weeks.

I can appreciate feeling uncomfortable, sometimes, because those feelings sometimes signify growth. I've avoided saying and doing some things I need to do for success with many parts of life, and when I write tricky ideas, it helps me uncover the truth in the process.

Is it a good thing people read my books? I don't know. Are they meant to be valuable only to me? Absolutely not. Because of their formation, I grow from them, though I still assert that things need to be beneficial for others, our world, and not only me. I have enough of what I need, yet I'd also like to have access to a car, a significant income, and more readily a girlfriend.

Two thousand four hundred sixty-nine words in two weeks is not an active effort towards working full-time on a profitable authorship pathway. About a year ago, I thought I'm to be a professional author, though I haven't put so much time and effort to do so always.

I have been lax, foolish, inconsistent, and apathetic with work, goals, and dreams. Even if some others say they think I'm active and busy, I know I'm not always. I've improved in some areas, though I've still had some hounding habits and behaviours that are not okay.

I may not have the same standards or expectations of others that I have for myself; I tend to expect little from anyone. I just think I need to plan far better than I have. Central repentance nudges me to remember I've not always put in work. If repentance is reverting the negative parts of myself too, then I must remember I need to correct and control my actions and behaviours.

I need to get to work.

ROBERT KOYICH

REVERENCE

I give this section, Reverence, as open thanks to all the forces that ally. Thank you each for allowing us to reach this moment and thank you for keeping us safe, guarded, and protected. Thank You for allowing us nourishment and nurturing, and thank You for allowing each a home in which to live. For those that don't have a house, please let them have one also.

I thank you for guiding me and letting me heed your warnings, lessons, and guidance. Thank you for granting me space and time to create, and I'm sorry for not generating sales of the individual fountains or actively searching for pledges. Please forgive me for not activating Full Seed yet and for not pushing myself outwards on street level to find future people with whom to share.

With reverence, I thank you for grace, and with trepidation, I ask you for prosperity. Thank you for keeping my friends and family safe, and in reciprocation for what I've been allowed, please allow me to gather, earn, generate, and share more than I receive. Please let me be a provider for others as well as myself, and for not having yet provided much for others, please let me make reparations.

Please allow us each to believe in ourselves too. Let us each find our pathways to shared life, love, and community with compassion, generosity, and kindness, and thank you for allowing us what we have. Thank you for allowing us to learn what we need to learn, and please let our wisdom grow to let us know rightly and justly how to understand who we are and where we are to go.

Thank You also for the forces of Heaven, and for the effects that protect earthlings too. Even if against biblical ideas, I thank You for not taking some from this planet too soon. I wish to stay on Earth for many more years, though please do not hold it against me for not seeking to reach the afterlife. Thank You in honour for allowing me to endure here on Earth, and I ask I may tend the worlds of life with a living legacy.

Thank you to my online mentors who know I've been lazy. I know I may not yet live up to your expectations, though thank you for your blessings, grace, and knowledge and for caring well for my ideas, my dreams, and our success. I apologize for not yet being a successful entrepreneur or business owner, though I hope some of your lessons and wisdom can seep into my text to also be in line with your missions and objectives. Thank you for tending *us* as seeds without having us buried.

For the girl who started the Fountains series, thank you for letting me release you too. I held on shackled and chained to my ideas of who you are without your consent, and I'm sorry for the negative attention. Please know I love you and let you go and that I wish you too may heal your heart. Thank you for the inspiration, forgiveness, and love that you too give and share; I hope you may find peace, love, unity, and respect also.

To the secret counterparts of whom I don't know, and am meant not to know, thank you for being part of the plan. Thank you for keeping us safe and secure, and even when I feel the edges of paranoia and conspiracy, thank you for putting my mind back onto builders and proponents for the collective vision as well as my success.

God, I don't know who You are, though I intuit how You are out there guiding each of us with sly psychic intuition not confined to only one dimension. You have been there in the past, present, and future, and I thank you so much for your influence and guidance.

It's humbling sometimes with my psychosis to think how mysterious forces are keeping us in line, and on task, with our purpose. I often don't know what my goal is; even with these books. I've struggled to force and forge meaning and earn my life with so little to show, and I hope my work has meaning and value; subtle feelings help confirm it may.

I also thank the churches, synagogues, temples, and

mosques that preach inclusive and non-discriminatory doctrine. Your work improves individual and collective lives, attitudes, and ethics. Religion is a crucial component of Earth and honourable and mutual respect for differing beliefs is part of how we may keep the peace.

For those that have passed onto the next life, I hope your spirits are well. I'm sorry some of you had to leave the Earthly realms in physical form, yet I hope you may remain active and remembered by those whom you loved. I hold reverence for you and the people you left behind. I hope you remind us decades later that the grief is a sign of the love held on Earth.

One primary friend of our community had taken his life in 2018. When I typed this, I felt the energy and power of his living friends and the devotion they have for him. I bowed my head in reverence and explored the significance of his passing. It's a forever honour, and the feelings I have are reverence for him and breathless shielding of my grief too. He and I were not close friends, yet the sorrow I felt for him is more than one might expect.

I learn how to adapt, and I accept a gruff reminder; I can't change the past. Before I started this book, reverence wasn't yet an R-word in the PLU8R philosophy, yet I comprehend its feeling and how it's in line with peace, love, unity, and respect. Reverence is respect with the delicate balance of order with love in regard for another. The unity part also amplifies the context for the person by the amplification of the power of life, grief, and love; even if feeling meek and alone in understanding.

How do we open our hearts up to happiness or joy when there are such things to remember? Some distract themselves and keep busy to evade the thoughts of loss or grief, and some others go to chemicals or food. The way I have started to choose to deal with my neglectful feelings is to get before the keyboard and allow the natural flows of text to unfold.

In an earlier Fountain, I wrote how the work is like a glacier. Snowfall after snowfall, I put my snowflake words onto the mountains of time as if it's a glacier. The more snow that falls, the more substantial the weight of the iceberg that may cleave into the ocean.

Is it my work is to bring the glacier down the mountain and return the snow to liquid water? Or am I trapping myself up in the mountain range amongst the hills with secrets held in the ice where no one else shall know?

"From the stars in the skies, the dove cries lullabies. Heaven vies for us to be free, while still held within the sea. The destiny we key creates fate to let us see, and yet set the net to thee for the facts of the ocean's notions and pacts of glee."

With reverence for some of our living friends, please accept us. I may not always share connection and communication as often as some would like, though please don't forget to call. Take the guidance and recommendation to reach out to people more often and don't have them be a passing thought. There are many friends that we may want to hear from us that might not make the first call.

It can be a stance to dance in life without death, yet death has a hold on the living. Some fear to die, while those living may fear for another's demise. It's not easy to be alive when we know some others are no longer here too. I'd gone decades without thinking of loss and the crossover from Earth to after.

And yet if we situate in peace, love, unity, and respect, we can endure with PLU8R. Friendship isn't always secure or there, however when we are allowed order and have passion, reverence can bolster unity. Respect can be an attitude and not just a feeling or regard for another after they've passed.

When people gather together in unity with respect, it's a great form of integration. Sometimes the connection can allow us to live and learn in love, so if we live to thrive, we may take heed of the spiritual realms if we have reverence.

I'm thankful I feel reverence for the living too and feel attuned to the truth when I slow down and grasp the significance. The forces of life and death reminded and remembered me to think meek and bold to hold on and assure we can give and care for those who also are a part of love.

If we can accept situations and circumstances, it's helpful. Remembering facts guide us towards the truth we must process, gather, and disseminate, and then our beings can attune to life. Life altering changes to our personalities are sometimes tricky, yet are vital.

I'm reluctant to call for us to play a character, though. It's because I don't think we should be playing roles; we should learn how to be with ourselves, others, and with the truth even when we feel uncomfortable. I ask, please, that we receive, accept, and learn how and what we are meant to do with our feelings.

Perhaps I should put more reverence into the freedoms I have found and formed. Through sacrifice, our current realities and society are shaped and allowed by the generations before. I'm fortunate to have a home, food, water, and technology that enable me to write these books, and for that, I revere the forces of life.

I repentantly think how I've been allowed to write these books, and sad I've not done more with them. I believe there are quality premises and ideas, yet how relevant are they? I may be redundant, or maybe the books are essential. I wish I knew when I write the works if they are valuable or a waste of time and effort.

Rationally up to when I typed this, I've not been relevant to others. I've written about so much in 'I' language and so little has yet had a substantial positive effect. Some have complimented me on my perseverance about forming Fountains; like my step-dad, Owen. Owen assures me these books are important projects. I trust Owen's opinion as he was a university professor and also is a published author, so when he says my books are important, it nudges me on.

I revere the significance of these opinions, and my intuition tells me they are valid. If I call upon these words for a purpose for more than just me, I must yield to the forces of life and allow the plow to dig deep. If these seeds are worthwhile, then I too must water them and be sure to plant more one by one.

As positive results manifest, I thank all who have assisted with this and ask you to let me know what these books have done for you. I haven't heard from many about how the books have affected them, and though not seeking affirmations or praise, I'd like confirmation these books hold value. Has reading this book been worth it?

What have I reminded you about? Have you shifted any attitudes and beliefs? Have you fortified some of your opinions or gleaned insight worth the time investment?

I can't confirm the worth of these books on my own; it's only a weird intuition that tells me they're valuable. I wish to be perseverant, not delusional, and when I don't know what the truth is, I don't want to make guesses or assumptions. Honourably, I'd like to gather what is right and true and plant more in our fields.

If the grains of truth flutter along the shoreline, then perhaps we meet. If the truths of our soul find solace, then mayhap we'll provide for those who need. If the voice is to match the beat, and time holds the rhyme as a cleat, then possibly it's right there's much more to write for you.

Two other R-words were to form as sections in this book. One is Redemption while the other is Renewal. I save them potentially for the next Fountain. It was time to go back to the revision process and release this book before writing those sections. I wasn't ready to write the chapter Redemption, and regarding Renewal, I'd not cleansed myself entirely.

I'm thankful and repent for how the Fountains have slowed. It was six months to form the base text for the 9th, and knowing it resolves, I feel gratitude, hope, and peace.

Please honour yourselves too. Reverence is not always from fearing another; sometimes it's acknowledging the person because we love them and those they know. Honour, admiration, and homage seem to be the trine, the three as one. If to continue living without trepidation, I best understand all three.

If we live boldly, safely, and rightly, then we also must add more to our attitudes and ethics. Let PLU8R seep into the lives of those we encounter with truth, honour, and respect, and as I give my pledge from the continuity of words and worlds of Earth, I thank you each for allowing us to make it this far into time.

I cannot assure I'll be here decades later, though it's a wish to reach the year 2053 one beautiful day at a time. We learn to intuit our creative and ethical guideposts and fortify the beliefs of what is right for us, others, and the world. It is imperative we continue to learn how to live and give, so if I can gather, atone, and reveal bright new parts of us to emerge, I hope to reciprocate kindness, compassion, and generosity.

I hope revelations of awareness can attune ourselves to beneficial pathways of life. May we develop and strengthen our resolves to thoroughly enjoy life and thrive. Let us understand and recognize each of the R-words, and perhaps it's true the creative instincts draw me to press on. We evolve and change parts of life into better situations for our world collectively.

Please care well for your being. It's not always easy, and sometimes it's necessary to rethink how we are living. I may overthink a bit much, yet as we refine the sand to silt, we get closer to shaping the future we want to live.

ACKNOWLEDGMENTS

Thank You and the worlds that coexist in this Universe. I thank each who've allowed us to be, and for our continued grace. I appreciate all who've allowed the forces of life, truth, and creative understanding that let this book manifest.

Thank you, Mom, Dad, Owen, and Sarah for the generosity of love, compassion, resources, and trust. Thank you, Chilliwack for allowing me to endure with the Fountains and for nudging and reminding my consciousness these books are for more than just our community. Thank you, friends; close, distant, and secret. I hope you thrive and find the desires of your heart.

Mentioning some of the online mentors and guides who've helped me in the past few years, I think of Gary Vaynerchuk, Gabby Bernstein, Lewis Howes, Jack Canfield, and Christy Whitman. There also are Dan Holguin, Florencia, Alexandra, and Brendon Burchard, and thank you too, Tim Ferriss, for guiding with your book The 4-Hour Workweek.

I ask we continue to develop the right channels for activating dreams with PLU8R. If *I* want to reach thousands of sales of my books, I shall need to learn how to react to high amounts of attention that a vast active audience gives.

And, for those that I don't yet know, though have read into these pages, thank you. I wish you amazing grace, peace, love, unity, and respect. Please keep your hearts open and glad, and I hope you also may find your dreams, wishes, and hopes become something awesomely real, radical, and enjoyable.

Robert Koyich – May 25th, 2019

The Fountains Series up to May 2019

Fragments of Intent (The Fountains of Yesterday)
Compiled from the first three Fountains
51% of Fragments of Intent's earnings go to Ann Davis Transition Society

The Sands of Yesterday (The Fountains of Faith)
A compilation of the 4th, 5th, and 6th Fountains
51% of The Sands of Yesterday's earnings go to Providing Point

Shards of My Soul (The Fountains of Fortitude)
A three-part book combining the 7th, 8th, and 9th Fountains
51% of Shards of My Soul's earnings go to the Cyrus Centre to support youth in need of love, safety, and education

Seeds of Tomorrow (the 4th Fountain)
100% of the 4th Fountain's earnings go to Providing Point to provide grocery cards locally in Chilliwack, B.C.

Fields of Formation (the 5th Fountain)
100% of the 5th Fountain's earnings go to Pencils of Promise who build schools and provide quality education

A Distant Glimmer (the 6th Fountain)
100% of the 6th Fountain's earnings go to the Dream Fund to buy things for people that they can't afford

Etched in Stone (the 7th Fountain)
100% of the 7th Fountains earnings go to the Friend Fund to share with friends who need additional support

Open to Fate (the 8th Fountain)
100% of the 8th Fountain's earnings go to Ruth and Naomi's; a street-level mission who give food and shelter

Sand to Silt (the 9th Fountain)
100% of the 9th Fountain's earnings go to Water.org who assist with supplying loans for clean water projects

www.Patreon.com/Introversial

RobertKoyich.com

Made in the USA
San Bernardino, CA
28 May 2019